FORGIVENESS
IN
ACTION

OTHER BOOKS BY HELEN KOOIMAN

Joyfully Expectant: Meditations before Baby Comes

Please Pray for the Cabbages: Pint-Size Parables for Grownups

Small Talk

Living Words of Comfort and Cheer

Cameos: Women Fashioned by God

Transformed: Behind the Scenes with Billy Graham

Silhouettes: Women behind Great Men

The Other Side of Divorce

Walter Knott: Keeper of the Flame

Forgiveness in Action

"Forgive as He forgives. . . ."

HELEN W. KOOIMAN

HAWTHORN BOOKS, INC.

W. Clement Stone, Publisher

NEW YORK

Dedicated to my dear and loyal friends,
Ed and Thelma, in whom I see
forgiveness in action

ACKNOWLEDGMENTS

Quotations from *The Revised Standard Version of the Bible* (*RSV*), Copyright 1946, 1952 by the Division of Christian Education of the National Council of the Churches of Christ in the United States of America, are used by permission.

Quotations from *The New Testament in Modern English* (Revised Ed.), Copyright 1958 by J. B. Phillips, are used by permission of the publisher, The Macmillan Company.

Quotations from *The Amplified Bible*, Copyright 1965 by Zondervan Publishing House, are used by permission.

Quotations from *The Living Bible Paraphrased*, Copyright © 1971 by Tyndale House Publishers, are used by permission.

Quotations from *The New American Standard Bible*, Copyright 1960, 1962, 1963, 1968, 1971 by The Lockman Foundation, are used by permission.

Quotations from "Divorce and Remarriage" by Lars Granberg in *Baker's Dictionary of Practical Theology*, edited by Ralph G. Turnbull, Copyright 1967 by Baker Book House, Grand Rapids. Used by permission.

Quotation from *Self-Love: The Dynamic Force of Success*, Copyright © 1969 by Robert H. Schuller, is reprinted by permission of the publisher, Hawthorn Books, Inc.

Quotation from "The Minister's Workshop: Rebuilding Marital Fidelity" in June 18, 1971, issue of *Christianity Today*, Copyright 1971 by *Christianity Today*, reprinted by permission.

Quotation from editorial entitled "Up from Suicide" in June 9, 1972, issue of *Christianity Today*, Copyright 1972 by *Christianity Today*, reprinted by permission.

Quotation from *Like a Roaring Lion* by George Otis, Copyright © 1973 by George K. Otis II, is reprinted by permission of the publisher, Time-Light Books.

Quotation from *Michael, Michael, Why Do You Hate Me?* by Michael Esses, Copyright © 1973 by Logos International, 185 North Avenue, Plainfield, New Jersey 07060, reprinted by permission.

Quotation from *Psycho-Cybernetics* by Maxwell Maltz, M.D., © 1960 by Prentice-Hall, Inc., Englewood Cliffs, New Jersey, reprinted by permission.

Quotations from *70 × 7 The Freedom of Forgiveness* by David W. Augsburger, © 1970 by The Moody Bible Institute of Chicago, Moody Press, Moody Bible Institute of Chicago. Used by permission.

Quotation from *Spiritual Manpower* by J. Oswald Sanders, © 1965 by J. Oswald Sanders. Moody Press, Moody Bible Institute of Chicago. Used by permission.

Quotation from *The Unique World of Women* by Eugenia Price, Copyright © 1969 by Zondervan Publishing House. Used by permission of the publisher.

Quotation from *Sinners Anonymous* by H. S. Vigeveno, Copyright © 1970 by Word, Inc. Used by permission of publisher.

Quotation from *True Spirituality* by Frances A. Schaeffer, Copyright © 1971 by Tyndale House Publishers. Used by permission of publisher.

Quotation from *Guidelines for Peace of Mind* by Dr. Harold J. Sala, Copyright 1973 by Harold J. Sala. Guidelines. Used by permission of author.

Quotation from *My Answer* by Billy Graham. Used by permission © 1973 by Chicago Tribune–New York News Syndicate, Inc.

Quotation from *Life Together* by Dietrich Bonhoeffer, Copyright 1954 by Harper & Row Publishers, Inc. Used by permission of the publisher.

CONTENTS

	Preface	*ix*
1	*Pandemonium in the Condominium*	*3*
2	*Forgive as He Forgives*	*12*
3	*Keep Short Accounts*	*17*
4	*Sad, Sad Words*	*23*
5	*I, Too, Was Once like Simon*	*33*
6	*Forgiveness Involves Forgetting*	*40*
7	*Hold Your Tongue*	*48*
8	*Are You Obeying the Second Greatest Commandment?*	*60*
9	*How to Be More Prodigal than the Prodigal*	*72*
10	*How Do You Make a Lover out of a Hater?*	*85*
11	*Paul's Strategy in Dealing with Hostility*	*93*
12	*Understanding Is Involved in Forgiveness*	*99*
13	*The Devil Wears a Familiar Face*	*106*
14	*Qualifications for a Man after God's Own Heart*	*114*
15	*God's Perfection Calls for Forgiveness*	*125*
16	*Heaven May Be Smaller than You Think*	*132*
	Chapter Notes	*139*

Preface

It would be interesting if one could interview one's favorite writers to determine the motivating factors that have contributed to their writing certain books. There would be as many answers as there are books. But I am almost certain that most of my writer friends would say they have written from an inner compulsion to put into words, on paper, the convictions in their hearts.

It was Joe Bayly, a coauthor of mine, who once said to me, "You write with a sob in your throat, don't you?" thereby articulating the force that has so often prompted me to write on certain subjects. But Joe was right. We (including Joe) who write with sobs in our throats do so because we want to share the lessons we have been taught from God.

I often say, "He is such a good teacher!" (What an understatement!) I don't believe God would have us waste any of these valuable lessons. When He entrusts certain experiences to us, is it not for the reason that we might help others?

The seed thoughts for this book were planted in my mind by a very new Christian many years ago. The idea lay in my thinking to be stirred up now and then by something someone else said or did, my own experiences and those of others, books I read, sermons I heard. I am deeply indebted to all who have in some way, knowingly or unknowingly, contributed to this book through conversations, sharing, or the writings of others (careful attention has been given to the matter of giving credit where credit is due).

My new Christian friend, with tears in her eyes, said to me one day, "Helen, it makes me heartsick because I don't always see in action the things I expect from some Christians. If I read my Bible correctly, then we are not to judge others, to talk about people behind their backs, to indulge in gossip. We are to be loving and to show forgiveness in action, aren't we? I hate to say it, but I'm afraid it's true—I have seen more kindness and understanding in some of my friends from my old life than I have in some Christians."

It was an indictment I could not dismiss lightly. She deserved an answer. I was one of her new Christians friends, and that day I pleaded with God to show me the areas in my life where I was guilty of the actions or omissions this new babe in the faith had described. I had to do some forgiving and seek God's forgiveness! Since then I have been very conscious of the behavior patterns in people that this new Christian friend so accurately questioned.

Special recognition must be given to writer David Augsburger and his remarkable book *70 × 7: The Freedom of Forgiveness,* which was the final nudge that pushed me into action—both in practicing forgiveness in action myself and in the determination that I must write on this subject out of my own deep inner conviction.

When I was a little girl, I would beg my mother not to bake until I got home from school (during the school year, that is). Not only was it a treat to lick the beater spoons and bowl, but Mama was always doing surprising things as she whipped up a batch of cookies, cake, or bread. In particular, I never ceased to me amazed when she baked banana bread. The recipe called for sour milk, which we never had. But Mama knew exactly what to do. I would watch in amazement as she mixed together some vinegar and soda and then stirred

it into sweet milk. Instantly, the milk curdled. Now Mama
had her sour milk.

I don't know why that impressed me as being such a wonder, but it did. Mama's secret became her daughter's secret.
While writing this book I took time out one afternoon to bake
banana bread. (What memories that brought back!) Sure
enough, I didn't have sour milk. The problem was remedied
easily, however. And then I remembered a conversation from
out of the long ago: "Mama, will your lady friends like your
banana bread when they come to quilt tonight?" (The big
quilting frame was set up in the dining room. Mama's friends
would quilt to their heart's content, and I would sit under the
quilting frame listening to their conversations and thinking,
What fat legs they have!)

Mama assured me they'd enjoy her banana bread. I'm sure
Mama didn't think her daughter's next comment was exactly
necessary. All I remember her saying was "Shame on you.
That's not very nice."

"Mama, your friends are like the milk—they look and act
awfully sweet and nice, but I think they're a bunch of sour-
pusses 'cuz they talk about people."

No, God doesn't allow us to waste our experiences, and
that one was lodged in my memory only to germinate while
this book was in process. Unforgiveness is the vinegar that
sours our Christian sweetness. Unforgiveness curdles the spirit.

HELEN W. KOOIMAN
Fullerton, California

FORGIVENESS
IN
ACTION

1

Pandemonium in the Condominium

She was heartsick. No doubt about it, her face clearly registered the heartbreak she was feeling. Her eyes clouded over with tears as I asked, "Jan, what's the matter? Would you like a cup of coffee?" All she managed was an affirmative nod.

I barely knew the woman. We were neighbors, both new in the condominium complex. We'd been casually introduced by the realtor's agent from whom we'd purchased our homes and had met and conversed just a few times. Her husband was of medium build, had thinning brown hair combed across his forehead, wore thick glasses, dressed handsomely, and seemed very intelligent. They jokingly talked with the fellows in the condominium office about getting a water bed. Beyond that, and the fact that Jan was slim, tall, and shapely and wore hotpants or micro-miniskirts with boots, I knew very little about my new neighbors.

Now we were walking past what I laughingly called our regurgitating stream—actually a running brook through the property—toward my place. Jan motioned to her house and said, "He's barricaded the door. He kicked me out last night after we got into an argument at a party. I left the party, and he followed me home. When we got here, he threw my clothes over the balcony into the alley and forced me to leave."

She'd used her last six dollars to stay in an inexpensive motel and had come back hoping to get into her home. That's when I bumped into her as she sat heartsick and dispirited in the condominium's office.

My son and I were on our way to church, but I'd stopped at the office first. Church would be home that day I sensed as I held Jan's arm and steered her toward our place.

She had no money left for breakfast, so we settled her at the table and gave her bacon and eggs and coffee. My eleven-year-old son, sensing her mood as she sat tousel-haired and dejected, wisely proceeded to try to liven her spirits with his funny antics.

She made one of numerous phone calls to her husband—calls that were to go on all day and on into the evening—only to be met with his slamming down the receiver each time.

"Jan, I don't want to hear the details of what's happened. That's between you and your husband. But I love you, and you are welcome to stay here until he sobers up and will allow you into your house." I suggested she lie down. She was plainly exhausted, physically as well as emotionally.

I was facing a critical book deadline and concentrated my efforts at my desk. With each page I breathed a thankful sigh of relief. The end was in sight. The current project had been a grueling one. The manuscript, page upon page, lay on my desk—a stack that was growing as the day progressed.

Friends called it a monumental effort, the most difficult book I'd undertaken thus far in my writing career. It was a biography of considerable length involving a great amount of research and many long nights of work (after an eight-hour workday in Los Angeles and a long freeway drive home) and weekends of seclusion where I did nothing but sit at my type-writer for hours at a time.

After almost a year of such a demanding schedule, which I meted out to myself with a discipline that I'd fought hard to attain, I knew shortly I could say the book was finished. *If anything happened to that precious manuscript,* I was mumbling to myself as the thought flashed through my thinking. Just as quickly I dismissed the thought: *Heaven forbid! Silly girl, what could happen to it?*

Jan was dialing the phone again. She looked at me, tears streaming down her pretty face. "Did you sleep?" I questioned.

"No," she responded, her face looking a little tense and drawn, "but I'm rested."

"Good," I said. "Let's walk over to the clubhouse and play some tennis. I need a change of pace and so do you."

An hour or so later we returned home. Almost immediately there was a phone call. I indicated to Jan to take the call. There was a brief exchange, a muffled protest from her, then she hung up.

"Mike's so drunk," she said. "Now he's cursing you!"

My throat tightened. "Me?" *What had I let myself in for!* But no, I wouldn't entertain fear. I'd only done what any concerned individual would have done—offered a little breakfast and a place for her to rest and make some phone calls. I still did not know the actual details of what had happened to precipitate the fight between my neighbors. And I didn't care to know.

Earlier we had carried up her nurse's uniform and shoes, which would need attention if she was to look well. She hung it in my closet and placed the shoes on the floor by the bed with her purse and keys. She would need the outfit for work the next day, and the rumpled uniform had been thrown over the balcony along with her other personal things.

"Jan, Kim next door has invited us for dinner," I told her. "We're going to share and eat up our Thanksgiving leftovers. I'm going over to help her." I left for Kim's with Jan reading the paper and looking wistfully at the phone, hopeful that he'd call to say she could come home.

As I was explaining to Kim what had happened and relating my increasing concern, Jan came bursting into Kim's house, frantically crying out, "Helen, he called, and now he's threatening *your* life. Oh, I'm so scared," and she shuddered.

We quieted her, and she told us between sobs about previous problems, of warnings from others that she should leave him because he could be violent when he'd been drinking too much, and all her inner anguish gushed forth.

Kim urged her to call the police and provided the name and number of a reputable lawyer to seek counsel. She refused. I suggested we call the condominium office and ask the realtor's agent to sober up her husband and to try reasoning with him. This we did. The agent assured us he'd handle it. We relaxed a bit.

Then Jan remembered: "Oh, Helen, I left your front door wide open. . . ." Her hand flew to her mouth, and she gasped, "What . . . what if he's in there now?"

"Look, I'm not worried. I'll just run over and lock up the house. Relax. Wait here." I left, and Kim took charge of the trembling Jan.

As I stepped past the front door of my home, I was gripped by a strange feeling: *I'm not alone in this house. Why should all the lights be on?* I walked to the bedroom at the far end of the hall and knew immediately that Jan's husband had been there. The closet door was open, and Jan's uniform was gone.

Had been there? I turned, and there, glaring at me, clutching his drink, was the crazed Mike. He lurched toward me, and I said calmly, surprising myself, "Mike, Jan's not here. Will you please leave my premises!"

He glared balefully at me, retreated a few steps, and said, "Get my wife out of here or I'll get you. . . ." He reached down, picked up her shoes, purse, and keys and staggered out.

I followed, locking the door after him as I leaned weakly against it. *Thank you, Lord.* All through the ordeal I was inwardly crying out, *God, protect me.*

After a few moments I climbed over the patio wall that separated my place from Kim's and entered her living room from the patio. When I told them what had happened, Kim once more begged Jan to call the police. Again she refused.

Later, after a dinner that all of us scarcely touched, we called the model office a second time. The agent, Frank, confirmed that he'd straighten out Mike so that Jan could come home later.

"You gals, I must write a few more pages on that book yet tonight," I said.

Jan and I left. Back at my house once more, I settled myself at the desk, and Jan lay down on the couch. The doorbell rang. I looked through the peephole. It was the realtor's agent. I opened the door, and he came in, glass in hand. "I thought you were going to get my husband sober," Jan said in disgust.

"He's out there." The agent motioned to the front of the house. "He wants you to come home now. He's okay. I've talked to him."

"I'm scared," Jan said.

"Jan," I replied, "we've been waiting all day for him to say you could come home. I think you should leave now."

I felt ill at ease suggesting it, but what was I supposed to do? She had refused to call for police help. My life had been threatened. I had a son to consider. And the agent assured us it was safe.

Jan rose, walking fearfully to the door, looked out through the peephole, opened the door slightly, then slammed it shut, locking it, and screamed as she ran to the phone. "He's drunk as ever. I'm calling the police!"

As she dialed for help, I sat glued to my chair, stunned at what was taking place. Suddenly, Mike was outside shouting profanities and yelling at Jan to open up. After a moment I heard wood splintering and from where I was sitting, saw my front door being kicked in by a violent madman. I screamed, and the agent ran out the patio door, leaped the divider, and disappeared into the blackness of the night.

The door lock broke, and Mike pushed his way in, ran to Jan, who was still at the phone, and tried strangling her with the cord. She broke from his grasp, but he grabbed her and thrust her into the fireplace. Again she got away, but he lunged at her, grabbing the gold chain around her throat, and slammed her against the wall. The wall-lamp shade took the brunt of that.

The next thing I knew he was wrestling with her by the big yellow fireside chair, and he threw her against a table lamp. There was the awful sound of more splintering wood and breaking glass as lamp and table crashed to the floor. She broke away and cowered under my glass-topped dinette table.

All the while I'd been frozen to my desk chair. Now I decided to make a break for help. As I got up, Mike came at me and pushed me around. When I ducked away, eluding him, he grabbed up my precious manuscript and flung it into the air. Papers flew in every direction landing in a flurry of white all over the living room. I was horrified as I ran out of the house.

Rushing to Kim's place, I banged on the locked door. "Let me in, let me in!" I pleaded.

There was no reply. What I did not know at the time was that Kim was on the phone calling the police while the realtor's agent was calming my son and her two sons. I was grateful my son was safe inside Kim's house, but now I, too, wanted safety.

Suddenly, I knew I was not alone on the steps, and I turned to see Mike stumbling toward me. I held out my arms full length and in a controlled voice I did not recognize as my own said, "Don't touch me. Don't you dare lay a hand on me. All I've done is give your wife coffee, food, and shelter. I know nothing of what happened between the two of you. Now please move out of my way. I'm going to my home. I assure you Jan will be out of there immediately."

He backed off, shocked into submissive silence. The ranting, raving madman just stared at me as I walked past him. When I reached the house, Jan was standing in the front hall, a disheveled mess, and no wonder, after what she'd been through!

"Jan," I said, taking her in my arms, "the door won't close, and Mike broke the lock. I can't do anything more for you. You'll have to leave."

"I know," she answered, more composed than I would have been if I'd just taken such a beating. "I know. . . ." She moved to meet Mike, who was now back on my steps. I pushed her gently through the door, then shut it as best I could, quickly propping a chair against it.

I didn't watch as they left. Instead I wasted no time in running to the phone to call the police. Then I dialed a couple in the condominium asking them to come to my assistance. After giving them the facts, I ran out the patio door, climbed over the divider, and banged on Kim's living room door. She let me in.

Within moments the police arrived. A thorough search of Mike and Jan's place and the immediate area turned up neither one. We did not know if she was dead or alive. One of three things could have happened, the police said: She might have broken away from Mike and was in hiding; he could have dragged her someplace and killed her; or they were together someplace.

I elected not to sign a warrant for Mike's arrest, which may have been unwise and was a very difficult decision to make at the time. However, in this instance I felt a restraining hand upon me. The police left after obtaining a report and assuring us that they'd continue searching for Jan.

Meanwhile, the couple I'd phoned arrived. Kim, the realtor's agent, and my son stayed next door. My friends and I stood in my living room, which looked like it had been through a hurricane. I slowly began picking up the papers—the precious manuscript. *How will I ever assemble them back together in correct order?* I wondered. While trying to explain what had occurred, my mind was concerned about the manuscript and Jan's whereabouts. Over and over again I questioned, "What could have happened to them? Where is she?"

The phone rang. My friend Jim said, "Get the phone in the bedroom, Helen. I'll listen here."

I ran to the bedroom and heard, "Get my wife out of your house or I'll kill you!"

I screamed back, "Mike, Jan's not here. She left with you." He hung up.

I hurried back to the living room. Jim was already dialing the police again. Minutes later the phone rang a second time. Jim listened on the kitchen phone while I went into the bedroom. The same threat was made.

Shortly thereafter the police arrived. Just as they walked in, the phone rang a third time, and the officer took one phone while I took the other. As he heard the threat made upon my life, he interrupted and said, "This is Officer ————. Your wife is not here, and I must warn you . . ." but the phone clicked before he could finish. Mike was off the line.

Other friends were called and arrived. The front door was barricaded, and the officers told us we could not spend the night in our home. My son and I left with our friends.

Later that night my friends and I went searching for Jan. More of her clothing had been thrown into the alley, but she was not to be found. The next morning, after I left for work, my friends found Jan running down the alley behind our homes with Mike in drunken pursuit. They threw open their car door and rescued her. They learned that the night before she had broken away from Mike and had hidden in a nearby model home rest room. When she came back and was picking up her clothes strewn in the alley below their balcony, Mike had come out and taken chase.

Jan did seek police help with the aid of my friends that day. Mike had pulled the wires from her car, but my friends fixed it. The police made Mike release her keys, purse, and some money. Jan went to live with a work associate for a week but later returned to her husband.

The day following this, as I walked into the condominium office, Mike appeared, brushed past me menacingly, and glared at me. It was frightening, I must admit. Still, I sensed an inner calm that assured me there was a reason for all of this.

On the second day following the episode I walked through the model office again, after picking up my mail, and Mike was seated by the desk. He was neatly and smartly dressed —and sober. Quite a contrast to what we'd been seeing.

It was totally unplanned. I walked over to him, extended my hand, and heard myself say, "Mike, how are you? You're looking better today. I think we should be friends."

He looked at me, disbelief registering on his features, gripped the arms of the chair, and struggled slowly to his feet.

I took his hands in mine, looked up at him, and said, "Mike, I'm sorry about everything. I love you, and I forgive you for what has happened."

Suddenly he withdrew his hands, took off his thick glasses, and the next thing I knew he was reaching for a handkerchief to wipe his eyes. "Thank you," he managed to say huskily.

2

Forgive as He Forgives

Forgive as He forgives. I'd read it all my life, heard it preached from pulpits, and quoted it dozens of times. I'd practiced it, too, and many times had found it difficult.

As I looked at the downcast Mike, sitting by the model desk in the condominium office when I walked through that day with my mail, I heard that still small voice within me saying, *Forgive as He forgives.*

Forgive him? The objection flashed through my head as I paused, momentarily stunned at seeing this man who had so recently caused me such distress.

Yes!

That's all I heard. And then I crossed over to him. Was it difficult? No, as I retrace those steps now in my mind, I was carried forward, as it were, on wings of love. Does that sound too pat? Contrived somehow? Or simplistic? Nevertheless, it's true. My steps did not lag or falter.

I reached him and touched him. Instantly, I knew there was healing in that touch; healing for this man whose spirit was so wounded. How many times don't we read in the gospel narrative of Jesus' touch, of healing, and then His words of loving forgiveness that followed! At other times Jesus would say, "Thy sins be forgiven thee," and then would follow healing.

Our Lord always placed the emphasis upon the state of a man's soul, his inner being. Physical healing was important in the eyes of the loving Jesus, but the greater need was to assure a man of forgiveness, of his being in good standing with God.

Whenever Jesus' critics, especially the scribes and the superzealous religious Pharisees, heard Him speak of forgiveness, they were indignant. "Blasphemy!" they murmured to themselves and each other. "This man is saying he is God!" exclaimed the religious leaders.[1]

The criticism of the critics never deterred Jesus from His mission. It made no difference to Him what people said, thought, or did.

> Jesus knew what they were thinking and asked them, "Why are you thinking such evil thoughts? I, the Messiah, have the authority on earth to forgive sins. But talk is cheap —anybody could say that. So I'll prove it to you by healing this man." Then, turning to the paralyzed man, he commanded, "Pick up your stretcher and go on home, for you are healed." [2]

The Bible faithfully records, "And the boy jumped up and left!" [3]

The reaction of the crowd standing nearby is interesting: "A chill of fear swept through the crowd as they saw this happen right before their eyes. How they praised God for giving such authority to a man!" [4] But not the religious leaders nor those who were unsympathetic to Jesus' teachings and the claims He made about Himself. There were many who simply did not understand, many who could not comprehend this man, Jesus.

Now, as I stood before this man who, only days before, had so misunderstood me and my motives in helping his wife, I felt nothing but compassion and understanding going out from me toward him as I recognized the inner sickness that had caused him to act so horribly.

"How could you?" I was to hear that question over and over again from friends in the days that followed. "I just don't understand. Forgive him after what he put you through?"

The questions tumbled out. Word got around fast in succeeding days. "Forgive him after the way he wrecked your living room?"

"Forgive him? Look at your bruises!"

"Forgive him after the way he treated his wife?"

"Forgive him? Look what he did to your manuscript!"

Questions. Surprised reactions and more questions.

But if Mike was shocked that day, the realtor's agent was perhaps just as shocked. My disappointment at his running out and leaving Jan and me that night in my living room with a raving drunken madman was pretty keen initially. Yet there was forgiveness for both. It was a forgiveness beyond me and my own capacity to forgive. But it was there, and it was real.

How do you explain the kind of forgiveness the Bible says we are to demonstrate? Words, I often say, are so inadequate at times. Forgiveness in action does not usually come easy, nor is it readily comprehended by the receivers of such forgiveness and those watching on the outside. It is especially hard for those unfamiliar with Jesus' life and teachings to understand.

Jesus was the Master Forgiver. And He is our example. What precisely did He have to say about forgiveness? And how did He measure up to what He advocated?

"Father, forgive them; for they know not what they do." [5] He was hanging on a cross—that place of cruel death and ignominy, between two criminals. Inhuman abuse had been heaped upon Him. The fury and outrage of His persecutors was, the Bible says, "fierce." He had been wrongly charged with nothing deserving or worthy of death, let alone bonds.[6] He was run down and hurried to the cross by a noisy, unruly, seditious mob. Pilate, the Roman governor, tried unsuccessfully to have Jesus chastised and released, but the people, the chief priests, and the rulers would have none of it.

"Crucify Him, crucify Him!" they cried,[7] and a mighty roar rose from the crowd as the people with one voice shouted, "Kill Him, and release Barabbas to us!" Barabbas was in prison for starting an insurrection in Jerusalem against the government and for murder.[8]

I knew the Bible story concerning this event and other events in Jesus' life. How did Jesus measure up to what He advocated about forgiving those who have wronged us? In the Gospels we see Him hanging on the cross between two thieves as though He had been the worst of the three. He was reviled and reproached, treated with all the scorn and contempt imaginable.

As we view Jesus upon the cross, we hear Him praying for His enemies. "Father, forgive them." Oftentimes, especially at Easter, we will hear sermons and read articles telling about Christ's last words. But they are truly remarkable words.

One would think that Jesus should have prayed, "Father, consume them." But no, He is making intercession for transgressors, for all those who spitefully use Him and speak evil against Him—even for those who hate Him without cause yet today.

"Father, forgive them; for they know not what they do." The greatest thing Christ ever did was to suffer upon that cross and then to die for us. He did it for our redemption, to purchase and procure for us the forgiveness of sins. This was forgiveness in action the likes of which the world had never seen, nor will ever see again.

But what did Jesus mean when He said, "they know not what they do"? There are those who wonder. Was He excusing them? He was saying that they, His crucifiers, had been kept in ignorance by their rulers. They had prejudices against Him instilled into them; they actually thought they were doing God a service.[9] Such are to be pitied and prayed for. Later, many of these same people were to fall under the hearing of the preaching of the gospel by Peter, and they, too, were to remember Jesus' prayer upon the cross. They, too, were to experience God's answer to the Son's prayer for forgiveness for themselves.

Jesus' example says to me that I must pray for my enemies —those who hate, persecute, or misuse me. Jesus' example reminds me that my neighbors are ignorant of His love and mercy, His forgiveness. If Jesus could pray for such enemies as would crucify Him, if He could forgive them, how can I possibly withhold love and forgiveness from anyone? Yes, even my drunken neighbor who threatened my life.

3

Keep Short Accounts

"Keep short accounts." It was my friend Marj offering those words of wisdom. They were like an echo from the past— something my mother had frequently urged upon us as being the better part of wisdom. "Always keep short accounts," Marj repeated herself and then went on to explain.

"This was so vividly demonstrated a number of years ago when my husband was desperately ill and we actually thought he was going to die. Word got around fast, and an old friend of my husband's heard about his illness. For years this fellow had maintained a decided coolness to us, and it hurt us very much.

"The most pitiful thing I ever saw was this man walking into our house when Warren was on what we thought was his deathbed. He came to apologize because he'd been carrying this grudge for years—ever since we'd gotten married— just because Warren hadn't asked him to be best man at our wedding. He drove many miles, came from a great distance, to ask Warren's forgiveness for something that should have been taken care of years ago."

How many there are like that—people carrying unresolved grudges like heavy burdens, struggling with unsettled differences, something that may have happened in the long ago, yet bearing the memory like a gigantic weight that presses down, threatening to overpower, and that, in time, can actually destroy.

What is gained by carrying a grudge? Ulcers. Insomnia. Elevated blood pressure. Muscle spasms. Neurotic disorders of all types. Actually, slow suicide.

Carrying grudges can be devastating. S. I. McMillen, a Christian medical doctor who wrote the inspiring best seller *None of These Diseases,* testified in it that health, happiness, and even longer life can be achieved by following the teachings of the Bible. He states that the moment a person starts hating someone or carrying a grudge, he becomes that person's slave. Resentment produces stress hormones in our body and can have a tyrannical grasp on our mind. The price we pay for allowing our emotions to control us strikes to the very core of our being. Our reactions to life's problems determine how our body will react.

"Is it not a remarkable fact," the good doctor asks, "that our reactions to stress determine whether stress is going to cure us or make us sick? Here is an important key to longer and happier living. We hold the key and can decide whether stress is going to work *for* us or *against* us. Our attitude decides whether stress makes us 'better or bitter.' "

And what does the Bible have to say on the subject of nursing a grudge and harboring hatred? Stop being mean, bad-tempered, and angry. Quarreling, harsh words, and dislike of others should have no place in your lives. Instead, be kind to each other, tenderhearted, forgiving one another, just as God has forgiven you because you belong to Christ.[1]

Paul is saying that with God there is forgiveness because of Jesus Christ. Who are we, therefore, to withhold that same spirit from those who may have wronged us in some way? Those who are forgiven by God should be of a forgiving spirit. God forgives speedily when we confess our sins to Him. He forgives sincerely, heartily, readily, cheerfully, universally, and forever.

In hatred everybody loses. The cost is exorbitant. A man or a woman can lose friends; a husband or a wife can lose each other; parents can be so alienated from their children they are lost to each other forever; a store clerk can lose customers; a professional can lose clients.

Resentment, carrying a grudge, has been likened to the cold medicine that is a twelve-hour pill, a capsule with all of the little grains inside so that at regular intervals another one is released, we are told, so the effect of it keeps working hour after hour. Resentment within us releases, as it were, these droplets of poison that circulate through our whole being and poison not only our minds but our physical and spiritual well-being.

A well-known doctor of internal medicine at Mayo Clinic for many years said, "I tell my patients they cannot afford to carry grudges or maintain hate." Then he went on to give an illustration of how he saw a man kill himself, as he put it, "inch by inch," because of a quarrel with a sister over a family estate. The man became so embittered within himself that his breath was foul, the organs of his body ceased to function properly, and in a matter of months he was physically dead. He literally killed himself a day at a time.

God has given us a timetable regarding just how long we can harbor grudges and nurse a pet peeve or be angry. He Who made our bodies knows full well what can happen when we allow grudges and grievances to simmer or when we brood over an injustice or wrong done to us.

In Ephesians the Apostle Paul says, "If you are angry, don't sin by nursing your grudge. Don't let the sun go down with you still angry—get over it quickly; for when you are angry you give a mighty foothold to the devil." [2] God is not saying there aren't times when we will be angry; we will be. But He places a restriction upon our anger. "Be ye angry, *and sin not.*"

We must be watchful lest there is excess in our anger. It has been suggested that if we would be angry and not sin, we must be angry at *nothing but sin.* We are to be more jealous for the glory of God than for any interest or reputation of our own. Strong words! We sin in our anger when we allow it to burn into full-blown wrath or we allow it to fester within our systems. Paul says the timetable of God is sundown. If you are upset by something at 8:28 and the sun goes down at 8:30, that gives you exactly two minutes to clear up the problem!

What Paul is saying is *Always keep short accounts!*

A woman relates that almost every night throughout the years of their tangled marriage relationship she pleaded with her husband, "Please tell me what you are upset about tonight. I'm truly sorry whatever it is that I've said or done to cause you anger." She quoted Ephesians 4:26–27 to him repeatedly. Most of the time, she relates, her pleas were ignored, and her mate lived in what she referred to as a "constant state of mad." Today this couple—a Christian couple—are divorced.

There must be many thousands of husbands and wives like that who have allowed unresolved differences to rise up between them until the invisible but nonetheless real wall is impossible to scale or break down. Complete forgiveness, on-the-spot forgiveness, before-sundown forgiveness, is the only way to root out the cancer of anger, envy, resentment, and hate that can hurt and destroy the man or woman who harbors such feelings. These sometimes subtle but pervasive wounds are healed by the Great Healer when we act according to His directives.

There isn't a single individual who can escape from the magnitude of truth covered in Apostle Paul's Ephesian letter written, as he says, while a prisoner in jail for serving the Lord. Here he was, imprisoned, with time on his hands. A good time for a man to do some reflective thinking. I'm thankful Paul endured those prison hours and spent that time wisely, leaving us letters such as this with advice meant for our own good.

Paul says, "Christ Himself is our way of peace." [3] Any feuds that may have existed in the past for which you have never given forgiveness or any grudges that may still exist between you and someone else should end at the cross. [4]

What shall we say then in conclusion about this matter? The respected commentator Matthew Henry observes:

> If you have been provoked and have had your spirits greatly discomposed, and if you have bitterly resented any affront that has been offered, before night calm and quiet your spirits, be reconciled to the offender, and let all be well again: *Let not the sun go down upon your wrath.* If it burn into wrath and bitterness of spirit, oh see to it that you suppress it speedily. There is the utmost danger of anger becoming sinful if it be not carefully watched and speedily suppressed. And therefore, though anger may come into the bosom of a wise man, it rests only in the bosom of fools. *Neither give place to the devil* [verse 27]. Those who persevere in sinful anger and in wrath let the devil into their hearts, and suffer him to gain upon them, till he bring them to malice [hate] and mischievous machinations. . . .

Has anger, nursing a grudge, harboring resentment, set up housekeeping in your heart and mind? There is only one way to rid yourself of it. Just as you go to the doctor when you have a rampaging infection in your body, so you must come to the Great Physician and allow Him to apply the treatment of 1 John 1:9. There we are told that if we confess our sins to Him, He can be depended on to forgive us and to cleanse us from every wrong.

4

Sad, Sad Words

Some of the saddest words are "If only . . . If only . . ." uttered when it's too late to say, "I'm sorry, forgive me," and a relative or friend lies cold and lifeless. I recall reading in my local newspaper about a tragic accident in which a teen-ager was killed. The mother's anguish was shown in her chilling words, "We hadn't talked for days. We'd had an argument."

In another incident involving the death of a child, in a school bus accident tragedy, the mother, when told, screamed, "I didn't kiss him good-bye this morning. I was mad at him."

Then there is the individual who is found lifeless, hanging by a rope from the rafters in the garage; or slumped in the seat of a car with the engine running; or with a bullet in his head; or the woman who takes an overdose of pills leaving behind a suicide note.

Suicide. Suicide—that's the whispered word, you know. But there are those who reach a point where the problems of life loom so large they prefer death. Suicide is considered the ultimate in the "geographic cure," but is it really? Actually, it doesn't "end it all"; it only changes a person's location. To what extent do unforgiving attitudes enter into suicide?

It is known that when unresolved conflicts and anxieties become unbearable, self-destruction seems more desirable for the depressed individual than trying to cope with the vicissitudes of life. Unmanageable difficulties are often the reason for suicide. Interpersonal relationships, stormy love affairs, broken romances, inability to make or keep friends—these are all determining causes in suicide:

> The most basic reason for the Christian's choice of life over death lies in the core of his faith. *God, who forgives* and accepts him warts and all, created his life. Good stewardship of that life which God gave and Christ redeemed—that is, living instead of dying—becomes a form of worship, a means of glorifying God, an expression of gratitude for the promise of eternal life.[1]

The Apostle Paul says:

> I beg you . . . to live and act in a way worthy of those who have been called [by Christ]. Be humble and gentle. Be patient with each other, making allowance for each other's faults because of your love. Try always to be led along together by the Holy Spirit, and so be at peace with one another. We are all parts of one body, we have the same Spirit, and we have all been called to the same glorious future . . . lovingly follow the truth at all times—speaking truly, dealing truly, living truly—and so become more and more in every way like Christ who is the Head of his body, the church. Under his direction the whole body is fitted together perfectly, and each part in its own special way helps the other parts, so that the whole body is healthy and growing and full of love.[2]

Unity and love, purity and holiness. Love is the law of Christ's kingdom, the lesson of His school. How do we attain to this high ideal which the Apostle Paul is setting before us?

The means, he says, is through lowliness and meekness, humility and gentleness, and long-suffering, which implies a patient bearing of injuries, of hurts heaped upon us, of wrongs done to us either willfully or unknowingly, all of this without seeking revenge, carrying angry resentment, and acting peevishly. A big order, you say, and who is capable of so responding? you question.

Paul says when we conscientiously practice this, we will build each other up, which means building up the church, the body of Christ here on earth, to a position of strength and maturity so that we are full-grown in the Lord, filled with Christ.[3]

Of course, this is a big order which we are incapable of responding to unless our lives are governed by the power of the Holy Spirit. And that means living constantly, ceaselessly, with the recognition that it is God's love, His strength, His power, His patience, His humility, and His gentleness only that is the enabling force within us. In our own strength we fail. We fall flat on our faces. We keep bumping against impossible, unscalable walls. On our own we are incapable of forgiveness in action which enables us to live joyously and victoriously.

Jesus gave us a pattern to follow in regard to interpersonal relationships. It is found in Matthew 5 where Jesus gives His great discourse known as the Sermon on the Mount. In verses 21 through 25a we are told that if you are standing before the altar in the temple (or church), offering a sacrifice to God, and suddenly remember that a friend (brother or some other relative or family member) has something against you, leave your sacrifice there beside the altar and go and apologize and be reconciled to him, and then come and offer your sacrifice to God. Come to terms quickly with your enemy (or that individual with whom you have a disagreement or with whom you find it difficult to exercise forgiveness).

How radically different the life of the church would be if

Christians were actually exercising such a forgiving spirit! How different life would be among family members if what Jesus said were actually being practiced! And what a difference this would mean in all our relationships with friends, neighbors, business associates, if we honestly lived day by day this way!

The verses that preceded this discourse spoke of being angry with one's brother. "Under the laws of Moses the rule was, 'If you kill, you must die.' " Jesus said, "But I have added to that rule, and tell you that if you are only *angry,* even in your own home, you are in danger of judgment!" [4]

Actually, God's laws are meant as a hedge of protection around our lives if we would only recognize them as such. What God has decreed, He has done for our own good. Christ is saying that rash anger is heart-murder. Anger is a natural passion, but it must be guarded and controlled. So often parents are angered at their children over things that are purely childish and cannot actually be helped—groundless circumstances, trivial reasons—when they should be exercising one of the great fruits of the spirit known as patience. How tragic for that parent to learn her child has been killed in a school bus tragedy, for instance, or an accident of some kind and there was an unsettled argument brewing between them for which no effort had been made to clear the air and offer forgiveness!

We hurt others and ourselves when we gratify our own brutish passions by venting our anger and refusing to forgive. This is a serious breach of the sixth commandment, Jesus says. For this Paul says we are *fools,* James says, *O vain man,* and Christ himself says, *O fools, and slow of heart.* The Psalmist says, *Bitter words are as arrows that wound suddenly, or as a sword in the bones.* The good name of that person against whom we have something is stabbed and murdered, as it were. The punishment for this, Jesus says, is severe.

We are to live at peace with others whenever a breach in a

relationship occurs. God's Word to us is that we should waste no time in being reconciled, confessing our own failure, our own contribution to the disagreement, and humble ourselves making restitution. There are many reasons why we should quickly forgive and seek forgiveness. If we are Christians, we must recognize that performance of religious duties, even offering of daily prayers, is unacceptable to God if there is anything between us and someone else.

There are those who question why their prayers are not answered. They quote Mark 11, which says: "If you only have faith in God—this is the absolute truth—you can say to this Mount of Olives [Jesus was talking to His disciples at the time], 'Rise up and fall into the Mediterranean,' and your command will be obeyed. All that's required is that you really believe and have no doubt! Listen to me! You can pray for *anything,* and *if you believe, you have it; it's yours!*"[5]

There is a qualifying verse that follows, however, and that is seldom included when one is talking about this matter of faith and believing prayer. Verse 25 says: "*But* when you are praying, first forgive anyone you are holding a grudge against, so that your Father in heaven will forgive you your sins too."

That little three-letter word "but" is freighted with meaning. But, you say, so and so has wronged me. I'm in the clear. I'm absolutely innocent. Though you may protest loudly and though you may be correct—someone actually has maligned your name, read something into your motives that doesn't exist, even scandalized your good name in some way—whatever it is, Jesus made it very clear (particularly in Matthew 18: 15–35) that if you have been wronged by someone, regardless of whether that person realizes it or not (and chances are they do realize it most often), you are to go to that person and get it straightened out.

Not only are you to pray regarding this matter of forgiveness and say to God, "I do forgive my friend for slandering my name" (or whatever the grievance is), but you are to take one giant step further and go to that person and seek to make amends. How difficult this is! And how few there are who are really practicing this way of life. How this would revolutionize Christianity in the world today if this were being consistently practiced!

The Old Testament prophet Isaiah recognized the truth of all of this. He laments the sinfulness of the people of Israel. God says they walk bent-backed beneath their load of guilt cutting themselves off from His help.[6] Why? Because of unforgiving attitudes, failure to exercise forgiveness in action.

God said to these people through the prophet:

> I am sick of your sacrifices. Don't bring me any more of them. I don't want your fat rams; I don't want to see the blood from your offerings. Who wants your sacrifices when you have no sorrow for your sins? The incense you bring me is a stench in my nostrils. Your holy celebrations . . . your special days for fasting—even your most pious meetings—all are frauds! I want nothing more to do with them. I hate them all; I can't stand the sight of them. From now on, when you pray with your hands stretched out to heaven, I won't look or listen. Even though you make many prayers, I will not hear, for your hands are those of murderers; they are covered with the blood of your innocent victims.[7]

Love, God is saying, is so much better than all offerings and sacrifice. God would rather we withhold our gifts, even our worship of Him and saying of prayers, if we are engaged in a quarrel or misunderstanding of some type with someone. Just leave your gift, go your way, seek out the person who has wronged you, ask and grant forgiveness, and then return to worship and prayer.

The Apostle Paul in writing to young Timothy, his son in the faith, gives wise instruction along this line. He tells Timothy that God wants men everywhere to pray with holy hands lifted up to God, free from sin and anger and resentment.[8]

I have been to many gatherings in recent years, especially

among those who are called the Jesus People, where I have seen young people standing—under the canopy of the sky at the beach, in a large tent, in both small and large auditoriums, in the Los Angeles Coliseum, at Expo 72 in Dallas, and elsewhere—with arms stretched upward, hands lifted, praising God.

There are many adults who misunderstand and regard this as pure emotionalism—and some say it's not so pure—but I beg to differ. I believe that these who are often so young in years and young in the faith have much to teach us who are more mature in both years and faith. I never cease to marvel at their sheer joy in the Lord, their unadulterated demonstrations of love for their brothers and sisters in Christ, and their simple acceptance of what God says as being the way to follow. I get goose bumps when I see those uplifted hands. I see peace on their faces. And love. Love and acceptance of each other and of us who don't quite fit into their mold.

"I love you, sister," they will say. And they mean it. God is receiving their offerings, their gifts, their worship. And He is answering their prayers.

There are men and women who refuse to go to church, or if they do go to church will not take Communion because they are at variance with a relative, family member, friend, or neighbor. But one sin does not justify the want of piety, devotion, and loyalty to God. The difficulty can be remedied easily by a tender, loving word. Those who have wronged us, we must forgive; those whom we have wronged, we must go to and confess our fault.

Just as we are unfit to worship God, to seek His answers to our prayers, if we are withholding forgiveness or not seeking forgiveness even though we consider ourselves the innocent party, just so we are unfit to die in that condition. Even as the mother agonized over the untimely death of her son in a tragic unforeseen accident, and another mother's child was killed in a school bus crash, so death can come to us or

someone we love in a similar sudden manner. We or our loved
ones or friends can be snatched away at a time when our
spiritual account with our Maker is not in good order. Oh,
the senseless, needless tragedy we inflict upon ourselves! What
folly to be so caught up in pride and willful stubbornness
that we are so insensitive to what we know God's Word says!

Agree quickly, the Bible says, while we are in the way.
While we are alive, that is. So long as we are at enmity with
another person, we are at enmity with God.

I recall hearing a young girl relate how easy it was for her
to memorize Bible verses. She was given Matthew 5:22–24.
Sometime before she had quarreled seriously with her brother,
and there had been no communication between them for
years. Now suddenly, she was confronted with a Bible verse
that told her to be reconciled to her brother. "What a difference between memorizing a verse and putting it to practice," she confessed!

I think, too, that as parents we must examine our hearts
in relation to our children. Many young people have been
caught up in the new, fresh wind that is blowing through the
church. The Holy Spirit is at work in a powerful, thrilling
way. There are those who believe that what was prophesied
in Joel 2:28 is actually taking place now. There we read—
and it is repeated in the Book of Acts—that God says in the
last days He will pour out His Holy Spirit upon all mankind,
and "your sons and daughters shall prophesy, and your young
men shall see visions, and your old men dream dreams." [9]

But many parents and adults regard with critical eye what
they see happening. They are censorious, even to the point
where they refuse to have anything to do with their own children or other young people whom they feel "have gone off
the deep end into emotionalism."

Hippie evangelist Arthur Blessit tells of a young rebel who
said he hated his father "because he won't extend to me the

compassion and forgiveness that he extends to the young people he works with at his church." The young man was wrong to harbor the hatred, but he made no pretense of being a Christian. He was unreachable, and someday that young man's father must stand to answer for failing to show love and forgiveness to his own son.

On the other hand, among the young Jesus People I have met who work with Duane Pederson, editor of the underground Christian paper *Hollywood Free Paper,* there is a simple, loving, very touching spirit of gentleness and a concern for parents and others who question their life-style and motives. The Holy Spirit is at work convicting them of sin and drawing them to God.

There will always be those who do not really mean business with the Lord—not only among young people but also among adults—but if we are going to say we believe the Word, then we must show it by our deeds and actions. God's Word says, "Be ye reconciled" before you worship Him or seek His answers to your prayers.

God, through Isaiah, told the Israelites who were disappointing Him in so many vile ways:

> "Oh, wash yourselves! Be clean! Let me no longer see you doing all these wicked things; quit your evil ways. Learn to do good, to be fair. . . . Come, let's talk this over!" says the Lord; "no matter how deep the stain of your sins, I can take it out and make you as clean as freshly fallen snow. Even if you are stained as red as crimson, I can make you white as wool! If you will only let me help you, if you will only obey . . . I, the Lord, have spoken." [10]

The time to begin is now. Today. Don't let another day go by without getting right with your fellowman or a family member—wherever he or she may be. Write a letter, make a phone call, pay a personal visit to that person. Remember, it is ac-

5

I, Too,
Was Once
like Simon

Frequently when I see a young woman with beautiful long hair, I am reminded of the once sinful woman who showed such great love for Jesus that she used her hair to dry his feet. Her story is told in each of the gospel accounts, but no one treats it with more dignity and beauty than Luke.[1]

One of the Pharisees asked Jesus to come to his home for lunch, and Jesus accepted the invitation. As they sat down to eat, a woman of the streets—a prostitute—heard he was there and brought an exquisite flask filled with expensive perfume. After she had entered the house, she knelt behind him at his feet, weeping, with her tears falling down upon his feet; and she wiped them off with her hair and kissed them and poured the perfume on them.[2]

What a picture this presents! The Oriental custom of reclining at the table while eating afforded this woman the opportunity to come behind him and do this. It seems that she might have met Jesus on a previous occasion and repented of her sins, receiving from Him His word of forgiveness. Now, having heard that He was at Simon's house, she slipped in unbidden where Jesus was being entertained as a guest.

She came to anoint His feet, but as she beholds Him, she is reminded once again of her sinful past, and in deep humiliation for sin she stands there weeping. Her hot tears of penitence fall upon the feet of Jesus. Quickly, she unbinds her long hair and dropping to her knees, kisses those beautiful feet of the Savior. Her tears are tears of sorrow over sin, and joy because of Jesus' forgiveness; her kisses are of adoration as well as affection. And then she wipes those feet dry with her hair. There is so much love in that act. Hair is a woman's crowning glory, and for her to use her beautiful hair to wipe away the dust and grime from Jesus' feet, which had been washed by her tears, was indeed an expression of deepest devotion and love.

But she is not finished. She had come with the special purpose of pouring her expensive fragrant oil upon the feet of the Lord. And now she does this. The fragrance filled the room, but more beautiful than the sweet smell was the sweetness of her act. None of this went unnoticed by Jesus, His host Simon the Pharisee, and the other guests.

How do you confess guilt to Christ? How do you admit guilt and wrongdoing to someone whom you have offended? In this woman we learn how repentance acts. There is more to repentance than remorse. There is remorse plus love—a giving of one's self. Her tears represented repentant remorse, the oil her covering of love. No truer expression could have been given from her of her gratitude and passionate devotion.

Simon the Pharisee stared at her. But his stare missed so much. The self-righteous person has difficulty in seeing properly. We might say the self-righteous Simons have a form of myopia—nearsightedness. That is they can see most clearly that which concerns "me" or "my."

The Bible tells us that when Simon saw what was happening

and who the woman was, he said to himself, "This proves that Jesus is no prophet, for if God had really sent him, he would know what kind of woman this one is!"

A Gentile, a sinner like this, a woman of such ill fame, with so notorious a reputation—these were Simon's thoughts. *How dare she even enter my house! But if this Jesus were really what He claims to be, He'd rise up with indignation. Why, He wouldn't even allow her to come near Him, let alone do what she's done!* If she had touched Simon, he would have backed off and said, "Stand by thyself, don't come near me, for I am holier than thou," and he thought Christ should have acted this way and reproved her, too.

The Book of Romans speaks much of being justified by faith,[3] and we have here a most profound example of this very thing. It is God who justifieth the ungodly.[4] Here we see Jesus speaking up, answering the thoughts of Simon, providing justification for this woman.

By His reply Jesus showed His ability to read even the secret thoughts of His host. Who else but the Son of God can do this? Jesus' words were a rebuke to Simon for his own impenitence and lack of faith. Jesus saw through this woman, all right; but what is far more important, He saw through Simon. And that's a pretty scary thought if you aren't willing to have your innermost thoughts exposed to the all-seeing eye of the Lord.

Jesus looked at the successful, pompous, self-righteous, respectable but pitiable Pharisee—this man who was so far from Him even though within arm's distance—and said, "Simon, I have something to say to you." [5]

In that look of Jesus there was nothing but love. Or should one say there was everything that denotes love and forgiveness? In sharp contrast to the way Jesus looked upon Simon, we see the way Simon looked upon this woman. One writer has suggested that when Simon looked at this woman, he saw her as a sniper sees an enemy uniform. He saw her as a gull sees a floating minnow.[6] Simon saw her with the eyes of a vulture ready to pounce upon its prey.

How do you look upon those who are different from you? I think back to my own experience with my now-married son. It was in his high school dating days, and he attended an Easter service with his girl friend at what we in our own church considered a very "liberal" church. How dare I impose that label upon that church? How dare any of us prejudge without actually knowing for a certainty all the facts in a given situation? More recently I became acquainted with the pastor of that church and his people. The Spirit of God is moving in a miraculous way—such love! My heart thrills every time I sit in on a service or talk to that pastor and some of the people.

My son returned from that Easter service full of what he had seen and what had taken place. He was thrilled; I was cold, unresponsive. I threw "cold water" on his enthusiasm. May God forgive me as I think back to that incident. (I have told both my son and the girl who is now his wife that I was wrong in my judgment and have sought their forgiveness.) It happened years ago, but I, too, was like Simon.

How proud and narrow we can be—like Simon. But Jesus has a lesson for us. He first gave it to Simon. It is the Spirit of God that is still offering reproof today. John's Gospel tells us He will reprove the world of sin [7] and unrighteousness. Paul tells Timothy that all scripture—the whole Bible—was given to us by inspiration from God and is profitable for doctrine (teaching), for reproof, for correction, for instruction in righteousness. It is useful to teach us what is true and to make us realize what is wrong in our lives; it straightens us out and helps us do what is right. It is God's way of making us well prepared at every point, fully equipped to do good to everyone.[8]

"All right, Teacher," Simon replied, "go ahead." Simon is saying, "Say on, Teacher, say on." [9]

Then Jesus told him this story: "A man loaned money to two people—$5,000 to one and $500 to the other. But neither of them could pay him back, so he kindly forgave them both, letting them keep the money! Which do you suppose loved him most after that?"

"I suppose the one who had owed him the most," Simon answered.

"Correct," Jesus agreed.[10]

Jesus was about to show Simon that He was more than a prophet; *He is the one Who has power on earth to forgive sins.* Because of this, by those who recognize Him for Who and what He is, He is worthy to receive what this sinful woman gave to Him—penitent tears, joyful, thankful tears, and the oil of loving gladness.

We who are obliged to forgive because of the plain teaching of the Word and we who are and hope to be forgiven can surely learn from this that we have an obligation both as debtor and as creditor. The Bible is severe in its warning that they shall have judgment without mercy that show no mercy.[11]

Here we have a picture of Jesus as our creditor, and we are debtors to Him. Sin is a debt payable to God Almighty. For nonpayment of that debt we are liable to the penalty. The penalty for sin is death, and all of us are guilty of it.[12] But God has made provision to pay for our debt, He has canceled it out, He has given us a blank check, as it were. All we need do is place our names on it: "For God so loved the world, that He gave His only begotten Son, that whosoever [can you insert your name here?] believeth in Him should not perish, but have everlasting life." [13]

Simon was a debtor, though the lesser debtor if he thought of himself (as it appears he did) as other Pharisees did. Remember the parable Jesus gave of the two men who went up to the temple to pray: the one a Pharisee, the other a publican. The Pharisee stood and prayed, "Thank God, I am not a sinner like everyone else, especially like that tax collector over there! For I never cheat, I don't commit adultery, I go without food twice a week, and I give to God a tenth of everything I earn."

Jesus, in that parable, said that the corrupt tax collector stood at a distance and dared not even lift his eyes to heaven as he prayed, but beat upon his chest in sorrow, exclaiming, "God, be merciful to me, a sinner." Jesus said that this sinner, not the Pharisee, returned home forgiven! For the proud shall be humbled, but the humble shall be honored.[14]

If Simon that day had a typical reaction—typical, that is, of the usual pharisaical attitude—then he thought of that woman as being the greater debtor. Whether our debts be more or less than some other sinners, it is *more* than any of us are able to pay. No goodness of ours, no amount of money, no great sacrifice—nothing can satisfy that terrible debt we owe. But praise God! He is ready to forgive, though our debt, like the notorious prostitute's, be ever so great. What an example that long-haired woman gave to us!

Let's listen to Jesus as He explains to Simon what He saw in her deed and actions:

> Look! See this woman kneeling here! When I entered your home, you didn't bother to offer me water to wash the dust from my feet, but she has washed them with her tears and wiped them with her hair. You refused me the customary kiss of greeting, but she has kissed my feet again and again from the time I first came in. You neglected the usual courtesy of olive oil to anoint my head, but she has covered my feet with rare perfume. Therefore her sins— and they are many—are forgiven, for she loved me much; but one who is forgiven little, shows little love." [15]

Jesus showed how keenly He had felt the lack of love shown Him by His host, and He contrasted it with the affection shown by the woman. Jesus is not saying that He pardoned her because she showed Him so much love—there is no such condition with Christ. Her love resulted from the pardon He had given to her on a previous occasion. She used this opportunity to show Him how much she loved Him; it was an expression of the debt she felt she owed Him, an effort to somehow give to Him, by way of her love, that which she had received from Him. Her loving much was not the cause but the effect of her pardon, His forgiveness.

Surely the woman noticed Simon's scorn. Contempt is not something one can conceal. Contempt is a betrayer to the discerning eye, especially to the individual, like this woman, who has experienced the love of Christ. Once you have been the recipient of Jesus' love and forgiveness, your sensitivities to the heart and mind of others are that much greater.

Perhaps a hurt look crossed her face, a look of compassion for Simon the Pharisee, but also, womanlike, her emotions showed on her face, and sensing Simon's contempt, she looks puzzled and hurt. Jesus looks at her with His great understanding heart of love, and tenderly He assures her, "Your sins are forgiven." [16] He vindicates her in the eyes of Simon and the guests, He silences her fears as she looks at these condemning, critical men. It is well to remember that the more we express our sorrow for sin and our love to Christ, the greater will be our assurance of His forgiveness of our sins.

Sin is costly. Be sure your sins will find you out, the Bible cautions; but know of a surety that there *is* forgiveness with Christ. Jesus loves to speak peace and pardon to those who turn from sin and sinning. We see Him in action doing that very thing in this incident. While the men at the table said to themselves, "Who does this man think he is, going around forgiving sins?" she *knew* who He was.[17] Jesus said to her, "Your faith has saved you; go in peace." [18] If you have such faith, then Jesus' words are for you also.

6

Forgiveness Involves Forgetting

Actually, the marriage should never have taken place.

How many such marriages there are! The reasons are varied. In most instances of marriage failure the couples did not seek the Lord's guidance in the selection of a life partner to begin with; they were young, immature, and unwise. Others, however, may feel they did seek God's will; yet often even these marriages go sour. There is confusion, questioning, and heartache. Many marriages begin in trouble—there is an unwanted pregnancy, perhaps, and so marriage seems to be the only answer.

And so the marriage began in trouble, was characterized by distrust and lack of respect, and unhappiness was predictable. Not always is this the case, but rising divorce statistics confirm the fact that not all marriages are made in heaven.

In B.'s case the marriage disintegrated when, after twenty years of pretense, he could not resist the attractiveness and flirtations of another, younger woman. After a time of clandestine meetings they were discovered. He was "brought to justice" by his wife and the dirty linen aired before business associates. The wife insisted on revealing all the facts to the organization where her husband was employed. Reprimanded sharply, and cautioned against any such future behavior, because he was a valuable part of the organization, he was told that if he returned to his wife. he would be forgiven and reinstated.

Forgiven? By whom? His wife? Members of his family? The many members of the organization? All the friends whom the wife also felt *must* be told? She had been betrayed, she stated, and others had a right to know what she had suffered and be aware of her willingness to forgive.

From that moment on his every movement was closely monitored. He had to account for each slot of his daily time schedule. He was a puppet on a string, manipulated by his wife and business associates. Made to feel like a person who could never be trusted and that he was indeed fortunate to be "accepted back into the fold," he felt less and less like a man and more and more in bondage.

. His wife phoned to check on him periodically throughout the day. He would report to her when leaving the office at night so she could time his drive home. He was subjected to a third degree constantly. When they were invited out, she told him what he should and should not say. If he tried to be funny—and he possessed a natural sense of humor—she insulted him in the presence of others and interrupted. When they dined out, she accused him of flirting with the waitresses. He was even accused of making advances to his daughter-in-law. Marriage became tyranny of the worst kind. Yet people marveled at his wife's beautiful demonstration of loving forgiveness.

Forgiveness? By whose definition?

This story is true, with much detail omitted, though it sounds like a poorly scripted melodrama. One wonders how many individuals—men and women—will identify with this gentleman.

Gentleman? Do you question the right for that respected term to be applied to such an individual? Of course the man sinned and wronged his wife and family. It was a grievous sin which cannot be overlooked, but he compounded his own problem by continuing to live a lie. The marriage was nothing but a pretense and a farce on a grand scale. A grand "Christian" scale to save face and preserve a false image.

He was a handsome, virile man, and his frustrations and unhappiness sought release. He was also a very creative individual, but he felt trapped. A man needs employment, and he was engaged in the type of work for which he was best suited. And so the pretense went on for another twelve years of agony. Every night when he returned home from work it was akin to returning to his own vomit; his wife threw it up to him ceaselessly. She could not and would not forget.

Is forgetting involved in forgiveness? Can there be real forgiveness without forgetting? The memories of the pain of another's misdeed may still exist—it does take time to forget—but if there is a supreme desire to forget, God can take care of that.

Just as God's forgiveness depends not on our feeling forgiven but on God's declaration of forgiveness which we accept on the basis of His Word, so the partners in a tangled marital situation like this who elect to stay together must declare forgiveness of each other and then accept forgiveness on the basis of each individual's word. But the one doing the forgiving needs to be willing to forget if true healing is to take place. Where there is an unwillingness or just a superficial effort mainly for appearance's sake, and the "offended partner" is unable to forget, then forgiveness is incomplete.

Regardless of how many times you may say to someone who has wronged you, "I forgive you," if you have not forgotten, then you have failed in forgiveness. If you find it necessary to remind that individual of his or her betrayal, unfaithfulness, or untrustworthiness, then you have not really and truly forgiven the other person.

God, in speaking through the prophet Isaiah, gave us this pattern for forgetting forgiveness: "I, yes, I alone am He Who blots away your sins for My own sake and will never think of them again. Oh, remind me of this promise of forgiveness, for we must talk about your sins. Plead your case for my forgiving you." [1]

Elsewhere, speaking through the prophet Jeremiah, the Lord declares, "For I will forgive your iniquity, and your sin I will remember no more." [2] And then, in the New Testament book of Hebrews, the Holy Spirit, bearing witness to those who belong to Christ, says, "And their sins and their lawless deeds I will remember no more." [3]

Forgiveness like that crosses out the past, buries it forever, and leaves it alone. It is to be buried in forgetfulness just as God has shown that this is what He does. Throughout the Bible we find that God has set a precedent for us by His own actions and statements. His way of action should be the pattern for us. God wants us to be as lavish in our forgiveness of others as He is. In addition, He expects us to be just as lavish in our forgetfulness. Unlimited forgiveness is His criterion. [4] And unlimited forgetfulness.

What about marital infidelity and forgetting and forgiving? Can it be done, or is this wishful thinking? Marital unfaithfulness is generally regarded as "scriptural grounds" for divorce; however, unfaithfulness need not automatically end a marriage.

Actually, many marriages have emerged from that kind of a messy situation better than they were in the beginning. Billy Graham has made the statement that to be successful, marriage requires two very good forgivers. In no marriage is this more true than one in which there has been unfaithfulness.

On the basis of conversations I have had with individuals involved in such situations, I am forced to conclude that unless there is a complete resurrender of both couples to each other and God, then it would be far better for everyone concerned for that marriage to terminate. Jealousy, distrust, possessiveness, and unforgiving attitudes are fatal to a happy marriage.

Often the one considered the offender is forced by the mate to live with guilt. Does God make us live with a burden of guilt? The Psalmist said, "If thou, Lord, shouldest mark iniquities, Oh Lord, who shall stand? But there is forgiveness with thee. . . ." [5]

I believe we have to confront the question of "betrayal" and who is the "innocent party." It takes two to tango in a marriage. On this subject, Dr. Lars Granberg, eminent counselor and psychologist, says:

> A comment on the idea of "the innocent party" seems in order. Any experienced pastor knows that it is rare that such a term is more than relative. Married life is an intricate tapestry of interwoven actions and reactions. Both parties usually contribute to misunderstanding, each in his own way. Hence the pastor is well advised to listen long and carefully and be slow to apportion blame. The more obvious offense is not necessarily the greater.[6]

Under normal circumstances, if a marriage relationship is what it should be at its inception, I do not believe that someone else can pose a threat or break up a marriage. Who has betrayed whom? Who is "the innocent party"?

If a man is receiving a banquet at home, why should he go elsewhere to get crumbs in a clandestine relationship? If a woman is being treated as she should by her spouse, why should she risk everything and search elsewhere for understanding, appreciation, and love? If either one is so demeaning the other with a constant barrage of words, undermining self-confidence and a feeling of self-worth, is it any wonder that the aggrieved party seeks solace in the arms of another who knows how to restore self-confidence and make him feel like a man or her feel like a worthy woman? [7]

This is not to excuse lightly those who have been guilty of adultery, nor does this indicate a lack of sympathy on my part for the one considered "the innocent party." But it is to honestly recognize that there is more to marital infidelity than appears on the surface. And we, who are supposed to be "kind one to another, tenderhearted, forgiving one another, even as God for Christ's sake hath forgiven us," [8] have no right to withhold such kindness, tenderheartedness, and forgiveness to *both* individuals in this kind of a situation.

Christianity Today magazine carried an enlightening article on rebuilding marital fidelity that has shed much light on my own thinking. The best solution, the writer believes, is to forgive the offender and rebuild the marriage.

> To begin the restoration, the hurt partner needs time to express his pain, bitterness, anger, hostility, or sorrow. Eventually, however, he must face the hard but necessary question "What have I done that contributed to this situation?" Because the extramarital relationship often supplies what the marriage lacks, the answer is frequently one or more sins of omission, such as taking the other for granted, neglect, failure to provide reassurance, negligence in expressing appreciation, or failure to be attractive, accessible, approachable. . . .
>
> When the offended partner realizes his own shortcomings and their contribution to the breakdown, he can, with God's help, begin to forgive the offender and rebuild trust. Although man's forgiveness is—like all else that he does—imperfect, both partners need to be willing to forgive as totally as they can. . . . He must also learn to forgive himself, something that is often harder than forgiving the other person. . . .
>
> Both partners will need to renew their spiritual commitment. They must cultivate their love for Christ. For the offended one, that love will salve the wounds and help cleanse

away the anger. The offender needs it to cleanse away the
sin and the guilt. Both must appropriate the Holy Spirit's
power: one will need it to stay mind and tongue in forgetfulness; the other will need it to maintain faithfulness. Both
need the fruit of His presence: love. . . .

   . . . A minister's wise counsel, pointing them to God's
example of love and forgiveness, may be the cornerstone of
their new life together.[9]

If you find yourself in this kind of a situation, the secret
to rebuilding your marriage is to forgive and then to forget.
It was said of Abraham Lincoln that his heart had no room
for the memory of a wrong. I appreciate what writer David
Augsburger says in this regard: "Now, let's be clear. Forgetful forgiveness is not a case of holy amnesia which erases the
past. No, instead it is the experience of healing that draws the
poison from the wound."

Augsburger goes on to say that you may recall the hurt,
but you will not relive it! No constant reviewing, no rehashing
of the old hurt, no going back to sit on the old gravestones
where past grievances lie buried.

True, the hornet of memory may fly again, but forgiveness
has drawn its sting. The curse is gone. The memory is power-
less to arouse or anger.

Not that the past is changed.

The past is the past. Nothing can alter the facts. What has
happened has happened forever.

But the meaning can be changed. That is *forgiveness.*

Forgiveness restores the present, heals for the future, and
releases us from the past.[10]

It helps to remember that with God it doesn't matter who
is right or who is wrong. He is reading heart motives and sees
through all excuses or attempts at rationalization. God isn't
interested in forgiving excuses; His intent is to cancel out our
sins! Jesus said with good reason, "But if ye forgive not men
their trespasses, neither will your Father forgive your tres-

passes." [11] Can you honestly say, "Father, forgive my sins, just as I have forgiven those who have sinned against me?" If so, then you are living in the manner we have been urging in this chapter—and truly forgiving those who hurt or offend you.

If, instead of reminding her husband of his affair, the wife had accepted the professional and wise counsel they were receiving and had worked with her husband to rebuild their relationship, the marriage that was mentioned at the outset of this chapter might have been saved. But in the end the wife's jealousy and possessiveness, and her failure to forgive with forgetfulness, destroyed the marriage. There was total, devastating disintegration, agonizing trauma, heartbreak, involvement of innocent others, needless gossip and scandal, and finally, divorce.

There was nothing left to salvage. Why? There was no forgiveness in action. No forgetful forgiveness in action.

7

Hold Your Tongue

We've all experienced situations in which we've been wronged in one way or another. And as long as we are in the land of the living we're going to keep on bumping into difficult, often irritating circumstances, situations, and people. A friend says he finds it impossible to get through a single week without getting into a little dispute with someone—his wife, their children, someone at work, a policeman, a clerk, a waitress, or a friend.

Life is complex and pretty explosive in our twentieth century. Sometimes we find ourselves the victim of someone's tongue, and word gets back to us about what's been said. Things get twisted and all bent out of shape; what began as an innocent observation on your part may end up as vicious slander. Much hurt and heartache can result. The pain is very real, the anguish great. To forgive or not to forgive—that becomes the question. Our humanness cries out for revenge, retaliation. Get even, something inside us says!

Is that the answer? There is a saying that goes: Doing an

injury puts you below your enemy; revenging an injury makes you but even with him; forgiving it sets you above him!

Forgiveness! "To err is human; to forgive divine." We do need to exercise a spirit of forgiveness constantly, don't we? Forgiveness toward our fellowman and forgiveness even for ourselves. And of greatest importance, we need the forgiveness of God.

I don't believe it's emphasized enough—the devious way the devil works through so small a means as the tongue—Christians who go around eating each other up. Christian cannibals, no less! Gossip, if you please. Judgmental attitudes. Slander and defamation. We play right into the devil's hands and become his tool when our tongues are uncontrolled.

It is difficult to understand how we can fall into this trap when we are so aware of what the Bible has to say on the subject, particularly James 3. More than likely our trouble is that we haven't read it or that we don't read it often enough —or if we do, we mentally pitchfork its contents over onto someone else. Here we read:

> Dear brothers (sisters too), Don't be too eager to tell others their faults, for we all make many mistakes. . . . If anyone can control his tongue, it proves that he has perfect control over himself in every other way. We can make a large horse turn around and go wherever we want by means of a small bit in his mouth. And a tiny rudder makes a huge ship turn wherever the pilot wants it to go, even though the winds are strong. So also the tongue is a small thing, but what enormous damage it can do.
>
> A great forest can be set on fire by one tiny spark. And the tongue is a flame of fire. It is full of wickedness, and poisons every part of the body. And the tongue is set on fire by hell itself, and can turn our whole lives into a blazing flame of destruction and disaster.
>
> Men have trained, or can train, every kind of animal or bird that lives and every kind of reptile and fish, but no human being can tame the tongue. It is always ready to pour out its deadly poison. Sometimes it praises our heavenly

Father, and sometimes it breaks out into curses against men who are made like God. And so blessing and cursing come pouring out of the same mouth.

Dear brothers, surely this is not right. Does a spring of water bubble out first with fresh water and then with bitter water? Can you pick olives from a fig tree, or figs from a grape vine? No, and you can't draw fresh water from a salty pool. If you are wise, live a life of steady goodness, so that only good deeds will pour forth.[1]

Surely, we need to heed what brother James is telling us in this passage! Hold your tongue, he is saying. The Lord of the universe is listening! The God Who made your tongue is bending low. What He is hearing from His children must grieve the Father heart of God.

The Apostle Paul talked about the fact that as Christians we are to be the body of Christ: "For as we have many members in one body, and all members have not the same office: So we, being many, are one body in Christ, and every one members one of another."[2] Have you ever thought, when you are misusing your tongue in talking about someone, that while you are so busy tearing apart your fellow Christian, Christ sees His body being torn asunder?

Actually such cutting jabs are wounding the body of Christ afresh "Who bought our freedom with His blood and *forgave* us all our sins."[3] One does not argue with God's Word. Do we not believe that "He is the head of the body, the church?"[4]

The story is told of Stonewall Jackson who saw his men fighting among themselves over strategy and the war. It is said that he jumped in and said, "Remember, gentlemen, the enemy is over there," and he pointed in the direction of the battle that was raging.

While Christians engage in verbal battle, cutting each other down with lingual mortar, the enemy of our souls himself makes inroads to defeat the cause of Christ. How tragic! Yet we have the unmistakable warning from the Word about this very thing: "Be sober, be vigilant; because your adversary the devil, as a roaring lion, walketh about, seeking whom he may devour." [5]

The Bible clearly states that Satan is the accuser of the brethren (Revelation 12:10). Have we forgotten?

How much better it would be if we were to act like those mentioned in Isaiah 41:6, of whom it is said, "They helped every one his neighbour; and everyone said to his brother, 'Be of good courage.' "

How much more effective is a pat on the back rather than a kick in the pants! The pat encourages—the kick knocks down. Self-centeredness recognizes no good in others; Christlikeness says, "Take courage," and seeks to refresh the heart of another. Chronic knockers, mudslingers, gossips, and backbiters are insecure, basically unhappy individuals.

Who needs destructive criticism or sarcasm? What an uplift it is to be around that person who knows how to speak kindly and shows tenderheartedness and forgiveness, putting into action Ephesians 4:32.

Life is difficult enough without Christians going around making it more difficult for each other. If David needed to pray, "Help me, Lord, to keep my mouth shut and my lips sealed," [6] how much more we need to pray that today!

But David also prayed, "O Lord, open thou my lips; and my mouth shall show forth thy praise." [7] Such is the balance we need. In a world reeling from violence and hatred, fractured by friction and people who have not learned how to forgive and who are being so wounded by words, the greater responsibility is thrust upon those of us who know better— whose mouths should, indeed, be giving forth words of hope, love, and encouragement and speaking of forgiveness.

The song of the critic is sour. His lyrics know no bounds. Such people seem to have an underlying bitterness toward life in general and people in particular. Others may have insight into people and their problems, but they have developed a chronic pessimism. Cynicism is often insight gone sour. I think we've all been around such people. They have nothing good to say about anyone or anything.

There is a fine line between constructive criticism meant to help another and that which publicizes the weaknesses of others in order to call attention to one's own superiority and "goodness." The Bible gives us a story that illustrates this so well.[8]

After the flood that destroyed everyone except Noah and his sons and their families, Noah became a farmer and planted a vineyard, and he made wine. One day as he was drunk and lay naked in his tent, one of his sons, Ham, the father of Canaan, saw his father's nakedness and went outside and told his two brothers. Then Shem and Japheth took a robe and held it over their shoulders and walking backward into the tent, let it fall across their father to cover his nakedness as they looked the other way.

First of all, I believe an observation is in order regarding Noah being found drunk. This is the only place in the account that we read this about Noah. He was a good man chosen by God to be saved from the flood and was not given to drunkenness or lying exposed naked. It was said of him that he was perfect in his generations (not sinless perfection—only God is capable of that—but a man of sincerity, goodness, integrity, and other virtues pleasing to God).

But look at his son Ham. To have seen it accidentally and involuntarily would not have been a crime, but for him to have seen his father's nakedness and react the way he did was another thing. He seemed almost pleased by it as he reported it to his brothers, as if he was, in fact, gloating over it. The observation has been made that "it is common for those who walk in false ways themselves to rejoice at the false steps which they sometimes see others make. But charity [love] rejoices not in iniquity, nor can true penitents that are sorry for their own sins rejoice in the sins of others."[9]

Ham told his brothers in a scornful deriding manner that their father was drunk and lying naked. He did it to paint his father in a vile way. The Bible clearly tells us it is wrong to make a jest of sin. In the Book of Wisdom, written by Solomon, we are told that the common bond of rebels is their guilt. The common bond of godly people is goodwill. A rebel's foolish talk should prick his own pride! But the wise man's speech is respected. To do right honors God; to sin is to despise him. A truthful witness never lies; a false witness always lies. A mocker never finds the wisdom he claims he is looking for, yet it comes easily to the man with common sense. The work of the wicked will perish; the work of the godly will flourish.[10]

We are not to publish the faults of others; we are not to expose them in any way whatsoever. Ham should have immediately done what his two brothers, Shem and Japheth, did —that is, he should have covered his father and not spoken of it to anyone. There is a mantle of love that we are to throw over the faults of others.

There are innumerable Bible references that bear this out. Permit me to cite one: "Continue to show deep love for each other, for love makes up for many of your [own] faults." [11] Yes, and besides this, there is a robe of reverence we are to throw over the faults of parents and others in the body of Christ.

We are to understand and forgive as freely and as greatly as God through Christ has forgiven us. There is stark reality in this unchanging truth when we consider our own fallibility and proneness to fall into sin. A challenging thought for our ugly moments when we are tempted to get even with someone who has talked about or hurt us in some way, or damaged our good name, is to remember that God sees us mentally naked—a fact that should drive us to our knees in gratitude and new resolution.

Thank God He doesn't expose us to the view of our family,

friends, and neighbors! If others saw us as we really are, how many friends and family members would we have left? Yet God forgives and accepts us. We are, the Bible says, accepted in the beloved.[12]

What a lesson this is for us! How do you react when you know of another's weakness and downfall? When someone whispers something to you about someone, do you expose it to someone else? Do you rejoice in it because it elevates you who have not slipped in this way? What do you do with gossip and someone's unruly tongue? What do you do about your own tongue?

Someone has well said, "Not even a fish would get caught if he kept his mouth shut."

We need to recognize that seeing and remedying our own faults is far more rewarding than carping at others and that it is vital to personal growth. Self-analysis and self-criticism can be a joyous and profitable undertaking that will yield far better dividends in the end than talking about others and exposing someone else's weaknesses and faults.

John Newton, profligate-turned-Christian, once said, "If my pocket were full of stones, I have no right to throw one at the greatest backslider upon earth. I have either done as bad or worse than he, or I certainly would have if the Lord had left me a little to myself; for I am made of just the same materials. If there be any difference, it is wholly of grace."

Someone else said something very similar when he wrote that the man who throws dirt always loses ground!

The writer of Proverbs said, "I will speak noble things, and from my lips will come what is right." [13]

Paul, writing to the Philippians, reminded them to fix their thoughts on what is true and good and right. Think about things that are pure and lovely, and dwell on the fine, good things in others, he said.[14]

There are many things we may hear and even observe that are true, but they are not necessarily of a good report. Paul says to keep quiet about it—don't even dwell on it except to pray about it, and then in the hearing of God only. If something is not of a good report, if it looks wrong, Paul admonishes that we are not to pass it on to others. Only as we comply with this will the body of Christ come together and be edified and grow.

Yes, our fallibility as imperfect people frequently shows. There's a credibility gap between what we profess to be and what we say. The Word tells us that because of God's light within us, we should do only what is good and right and true.[15] We will be judged on whether or not we are doing what Christ wants us to do. We are to watch what we do (say) and what we think.[16]

We have become so proficient at carefully calculated innuendos. It is frightening. The subtle disparagements we make about others are inconsistent with the truth we profess to believe. I could not agree more with anyone than with Dr. Carl F. H. Henry, writing in the magazine *Christianity Today:*

> If you are not satisfied with the way E. Stanley Jones, or Billy Graham, or this present lesser luminary, holds out hope to this present generation, then for heaven's sake, for God's sake and the Gospel's sake, don't exhaust your energies in indexing their faults—which are many—but light a brighter light and live a life of great power.[17]

What is the remedy to this age-old evil of misusing our tongues? We need to see it for what it really is—a practice contrary to the very spirit of the gospel. We need to forgive it in others, and admit it and forgive ourselves for it and go on from there determined with God's help not to succumb to the drag of the tempter in this regard again. And when we do, we must immediately confess it and seek God's forgiveness.

Several things are necessary if we are to escape this quagmire. First, we must have a love for people. We need to concentrate on 1 Corinthians 13 agape-type love and to realize that our own virtues amount to an absolute nothing in God's sight if we are not practicing that kind of all-encompassing love. No wonder Henry Drummond, writing in the masterful book *The Greatest Thing in the World,* said, "What we are stretches past what we do, beyond what we possess."

This does not mean that we will gloss over the faults and weaknesses of others, but it means that we will exercise love, forgiveness, and understanding toward them. We will endeavor to help them. We will recognize that there are some things that are better left unsaid. True love is more ready to sympathize with another's weaknesses than to publicize them. We must try to help others, to bring about a healing in their own person. We must protect, restore, cover the sins and weaknesses of others and always point them to Christ. One of the true tests of a Christlike character is seen in your attitude and mine to another's sin.

"If you know something that would hinder or hurt the life or reputation of another, bury it. Forget it. End it right there. It will rest in peace. So will you." [18]

If you "love your neighbor," remember, "Love covers a multitude of sins." [19]

Love can even remove a beam of malice from a critical eye. Love heals. Love encourages. Love protects. Love looks for the best in others so that others may be their best.

"Vow never to pass on anything about anybody else that will hurt him in any way." [20]

The real remedy has been given by Jesus. He said:

> Don't criticize, and then you won't be criticized. For others will treat you as you treat them. And why worry about a speck in the eye of a brother when you have a board in your own? Should you say, "Friend, let me help you get that speck out of your eye," when you can't even see because of the board in your own? Hypocrite! First get rid of the board. Then you can see to help your brother.[21]

Summarizing these words of Christ, William Barclay suggests three reasons why no one can judge another:

1. We never know the whole facts or the whole person.
2. It is almost impossible for any man to be strictly impartial in his judgment.
3. No man is good enough to judge any other man. Our own faults and our own inability to resolve them automatically disqualify us as fair critics.

The question may arise in your thinking, What of those times, however, when a person must make a judgment? What then? The Bible gives us the answer to that, too. Galatians 6:1 tells us. "Brethren, if a man be overtaken in a fault, ye which are spiritual restore such an one in the spirit of meekness; considering thyself, lest thou also be tempted."

> Judge and criticize lovingly—for the purpose of helping, lifting, and redeeming. Not to punish or get even. After all, that's the kind of merciful, compassionate love God showed us in Jesus Christ. And Jesus Christ gives that same strength to love and forgive to all those who open their lives to Him, risking the label, 'Christian,' to follow Him in daily life.[22]

John and Charles Wesley, founding fathers of the Wesleyan movement, drew up six points that they subscribed to in this regard. What a blessed thing it would be if each of us would try to follow them:

1. That we will not listen to, or willingly enquire after, any ill concerning each other.
2. That if we do hear any ill of each other we will not be forward to believe it.
3. That as soon as possible we will communicate what we hear, by speaking or writing to the person concerned.

4. That till we have done this, we will not write or speak a syllable of it to any person whatsoever.
5. That neither will we mention it, after we have done this, to any other person whatsoever.
6. That we will not make any exception to these rules, unless we think ourselves absolutely obliged in conscience to do so.

The wise writer of still another era, Thomas a Kempis, wrote: "In judging others, a man labors to no purpose, commonly errs, and easily sins; but in examining himself, he is always wisely and usefully employed."

Then, to keep from being dragged down and caught in misuse of our tongues, we need a greater concept of God's sovereignty, the fact that He is still in control of man and this universe. We are bound to see organizations and individuals with fatal flaws in their makeup and personalities and organizational structure. They will have atrocious weaknesses. But we need not succumb to an attitude of hopelessness, as if God has been defeated.

God is still on the throne; Jesus is still interceding; and the Holy Spirit is still at work convicting men of their sins and their need of cleansing and the work of His power in their lives. If God can forgive and accept them, so can we. Man's corrupt sinful nature comes as no surprise to Almighty God. Can we not be thankful that God has been able to accomplish as much as He has through fallen humanity? He is the one Who "worketh all things after the counsel of His own will." [23]

Yes, we are to be discerning and work the work of the Father while there is yet time, as the Bible admonishes. But we are to do all things in the spirit of love and forgiveness that Jesus has demonstrated so beautifully in His life upon earth.

And finally, we need to forgive ourselves for the gossiping, the slander, the abusiveness, we have heaped upon others with our tongue. God is concerned about our tongues. He wants us to have good speech. He says, "A wholesome tongue is a tree of life." [24]

The Bible instructs us to let our speech be always with grace (pleasant and winsome), seasoned (as it were) with salt, that we may know how to answer every man. [25]

The human emotional makeup is very delicate. We are bruised so easily by careless words. Words are powerful, both for building someone up and for tearing him down. We must discipline our tongues lest we become a pawn in Satan's hand to wound others. If we know we have done this, then we must quickly seek forgiveness from the one we have so injured; and then we must quickly forgive ourselves.

Forgive ourselves. That's a subject for an entire new chapter.

8

Are You Obeying the Second Greatest Commandment?

You are to love yourself. Wait just a minute, you say, such conceit. Such arrogance. How vain can you be? What do you think I am, anyway—a self-centered egotistical snob? Before you back off any further from reading this chapter or throwing the whole book aside, give the Bible a chance. Not me or what I am trying to say, but give God's Word a chance.

Jesus once told the self-righteous Pharisees who were trying to trip him up (a favorite pastime of theirs, by the way) that their errors (in thinking and acting) were caused by their ignorance of the Scriptures and of God's power![1] Pretty potent words those. Especially to use on men who were supposed to be so learned in the Scriptures, men who were known to have *the* answers.

Actually, their talk and actions were two different things. Their practice was in no way compatible with their preaching or their profession. Jesus said it, and I fear He can still say it today. He said, "They say and do not."[2] Their conversation gives them the lie. But ignorance of the Scriptures gives rise

to much heartache and grief. And we need a proper understanding of the Word to do what God commands.

The Bible tells us that the crowds of people who gathered
around Jesus were profoundly impressed by his answers to
the questions of the learned men of the law. He surprised and
baffled the Pharisees and routed the Sadducees with his re-
plies.[3] Dr. Robert H. Schuller says:

> It is interesting that the only persons ever accused of
> being horrible sinners by Christ were the very narrow-
> minded, legalistic, hyperreligious people. "A generation of
> vipers," He called them.
>
> What did they do that was so hellish? Under the guise of
> authoritarian religion, they destroyed man's sense of self-
> affection and self-worth. Perhaps nothing destroys one's sense
> of self-respect more than the finger-pointing, wrist-slapping,
> fist-shaking religious authority which claims to speak in the
> name of God.
>
> Dr. Samuel Shoemaker, a prominent American church-
> man, said, "Religion can never be the answer to human prob-
> lems. All of the religions of the world are inadequate. Christ
> alone is the answer. Christ alone understands. Christ alone
> forgives. Christ alone eliminates your guilt. Christ alone
> saves and then assures you that you are God's child and the
> most wonderful person possible! Christ alone fills the hu-
> man heart with love—joy—peace—self-confidence. No won-
> der a genuine Christian really loves himself.[4]

Yes, you are to love yourself, and it's a completely biblical
statement. In fact, it's the second commandment. Listen to
what Jesus said in answer to the lawyer who asked him,
"Which is the most important command in the laws of
Moses?"

Jesus replied, "Love the Lord your God with all your
heart, soul, and mind. This is the first and greatest commandment. The second most important is similar: Love your neighbor as much as you love yourself. All the other command-
ments and all the demands of the prophets stem from these

two laws and are fulfilled if you obey them. Keep only these and you will find that you are obeying all the others." [5]

This puts loving yourself in the right perspective. How can you possibly treat your neighbor right, how can you possibly love your neighbor (family members, relatives, friends, anyone), unless you have a proper, healthy, balanced love of self? Hate yourself and you'll hate others. All of the law is fulfilled in one word, and that is *love*. Love for God, others, and self.

The Apostle Paul caught the implication of what Jesus commanded. He said:

> Pay all your debts except the debt of love for others—never finish paying that! For if you love them, you will be obeying all of God's laws, fulfilling all his requirements. If you love your neighbor as much as you love yourself, you will not want to harm or cheat him, or kill him or steal from him. And you won't sin with his wife or want what is his, or do anything else the Ten Commandments say is wrong. All ten are wrapped up in this one, to love your neighbor as you love yourself. Love does no wrong to anyone. That's why it fully satisfies all of God's requirements. It is the only law you need. [6]

We are creatures cut out for love. God has made us that way, no use denying it. Love is a short and sweet word. It cannot be denied that there is a self-love that is corrupt and to be despised; but Christ is here teaching a self-love that is both natural and right. You are to regard with due dignity your own self; you are to take care of yourself. This kind of self-love is another fruit of faith.

In more than a dozen places the Bible gives the command to love ourselves. Do nothing to demean your own character. Hold yourself in a healthy high regard just as Christ taught, but remember, don't hold yourself any higher than you hold your neighbor.

There are many people, however, who hate themselves.

I appreciate so much the words that my friend, George Otis, has written about this phenomenon. He says:

> Hatred of self is so subtle in its workings. We have a stealthy foe who tries to turn something noble into something base. We know that God is pleased when we have a humble and contrite heart. The pride of life and egotism erodes character. It is good to esteem others more highly than ourselves. But Satan will try to turn even this against us if we let him.
>
> Don't ever let Satan get you to demeaning yourself. He is the false accuser and he tries to accentuate the negative. He wants to get you on a train of thought so that you deplore your attributes. He likes to get you to peer into the mirror hating yourself. When self-debasing starts to come in, cast it down. Instead thank and praise God for every good thing about yourself. Your eyes, a sound mind, and so forth. Inventory your many blessings and that depressing spirit that Satan fostered will go. When allowed to diabolically progress it takes the form of self-destruction.[7]

This is certainly very true and can be proved in many cases of suicide and would-be suicides—people who cannot, for one reason or other, love and forgive themselves for misdeeds, real or imagined. And the enemy of our souls is ever wary for people like this and will pounce upon such individuals using this weakness to ensnare and destroy them. To be aware of this is to be forewarned and ready to rout the attacker.

Are you beginning to understand better now why you are to cultivate a healthy self-love? Mr. Otis has this also to say on the subject:

> God made just one of you, and He made you for His own pleasure. Then He broke the mold—you are wonderfully unique to Him. He loves you with the same intensity and divine passion that He does the most brilliant, or beautiful, or noble person you have ever seen. You have been fearfully and wonderfully made in His image. You are a

child of the King—literal royalty—and don't you forget it!
Don't be negative concerning any aspect of your person in
the guise of humility. How dare we call "common" that
which God has made! Do you see it? Don't open yourself to
tormenting thoughts about unattractiveness, inadequacy, or
general self-abasement. These are from your adversary. Reject such thoughts in the name of Jesus. Praise God for
you! [8]

What is it that causes people to hate themselves or to have
a low self-image? It is generally believed that depressing guilt,
which is a condemning conscience, contributes more than anything else to feelings of fear, lonely emptiness, hostility toward
self, and feelings of inadequacy and unworthiness. Guilty people are love-starved people—loving neither themselves nor
others. And what, then, does this do to their professed love
of God? Certainly, the guilt is compounded.

These are people who cannot forgive themselves. And again,
on the basis of what the Bible says, we are justified in asking,
What, then, does this do to their forgiveness of others? And
it goes without saying that they also suffer greatly for fear
they are not totally forgiven by God.

What a vicious circle this is. No wonder God commands
us to love ourselves. No wonder He said to forgive others as
you wish to be forgiven.[9] How important it is to take what
the Bible says and live by it!

This is borne out in conversations I have had with pastors
while researching for this book and in the "My Answer" column, by Billy Graham, which appears in our local evening
paper. I have also frequently seen letters in the "Ann Land-
ers" and "Dear Abby" columns that speak to this subject of
guilt and the inability to forgive one's self.

Someone wrote to the "My Answer" column and questioned:

> I got married at 16, had a child at 17, and ran away with
> a married man at 19. We each got a divorce, and married sev-

eral years later. Now we've been together almost 40 years but guilt has been my constant companion. Often, I've thought of running. Lately though, I've felt an urgency to change our lives. Can we be forgiven and find happiness in these remaining years?

A sob caught in my throat as I read that! What a needless waste—forty years of carrying a useless burden of guilt.

Billy Graham's answer read like this:

Forgiveness and happiness are what the Gospel is all about! What you report recently as a feeling of dissatisfaction with the past, and a longing for something better, could well be the impact of God's Spirit working in your life. This is His business—to show us our shortcomings and point to their remedy in Christ. That is your first and greatest need.

Guilt is one of the most destructive forces in life. It can erode hope, smash dreams, and constantly give cause for anxiety. We can push it into our subconscious, but only God can push it aside forever.

God's plan through faith in Christ His Son, was that we be relieved of guilt. No wonder the hymn asserts: "He breaks the power of canceled sin—He sets the prisoner free." If we perpetuate the memory of our mistakes, after God has forgiven and forgotten them, we do a great disservice to ourselves, not to mention God.

Certainly no good purpose would be served by running away. Take your life as it is now. Let the past be the past. Live each day with a conscious commitment to God—and to your husband. With this preoccupation, happiness will surely come.

A minister friend relates several very sad stories that show the great damage that we incur to our emotional and physical well-being when we harbor guilt and are unable to forgive ourselves. He tells of a vacationing family who were pulling a trailer behind their car. The wife asked the husband to stop at a trailer park—she was tired and so were the children—

but the husband wanted to go just a little farther, and so they went on. Not too far down the road the axle on the trailer broke, and in the ensuing accident their four-year-old son was killed. To this day the father blames himself for his son's death. He cannot forgive himself for failing to heed his wife's request.

This same minister also told me—and this could be repeated with varying circumstances by thousands of ministers and counselors—of the happily married couple who discovered that the wife had a serious heart defect. Two things could be done: She could spend the rest of her life in a wheelchair, or she could submit to an operation that would restore her to full, normal health provided the surgery was successful.

The chances for surgical failure, it was felt, were very remote. The husband and wife prayed about it, and then the decision was left to the wife. She elected to have the operation, and her husband signed the consent agreement. But the unlikely happened, that slim possibility of failure occurred, and the woman died on the operating table. The husband lives with a haunting sense of guilt—he cannot forgive himself.

There are many people like the woman who unburdened her heart and said, "Fifteen years ago I disobeyed God's command and committed adultery. My husband has forgiven me, but I just can't seem to find peace of mind. I can't seem to think of anything else. What can I do?"

She had earnestly sought and received God's forgiveness, and her husband had forgiven her, but she had not forgiven herself.

Then there is the twenty-four-year-old woman who wrote to a radio pastor saying she'd been divorced and in the one year since the divorce was final she had been to bed with five different men. She, too, had confessed it to God and was seeking to live differently, but she could not forgive herself either.

The Psalmist who sinned grievously and even had another man put into the line of battle where he was killed so he could have the man's wife (whom he had already taken), knew what it was to experience God's forgiveness. He could say that God removes our sins as far as the east is from the west. He forgives all my sins, said David, and He heals me.[10]

There's the key, the clue, the missing link—God forgives *and* heals. To free us from incriminating guilt, we need God's healing of our condemning conscience. Forgiveness of self follows as a natural result. Such forgiveness liberates our hearts from enslaving emotions and attitudes.

Dr. Harold J. Sala offers this suggestion to help one forgive one's self. He says:

> Picture your sins that have created separation from God and brought guilt to your soul as written on a sign, and nailed to the old rugged cross upon which Jesus was crucified. But picture those sins of yours covered, blotted out with the precious blood that flowed from the veins of God's only Son.
>
> This is the very picture that Paul used to show the Colossians that God's forgiveness is complete. He said God has forgiven all our trespasses, "blotting out the handwriting of ordinances that was against us, which was contary to us, and took it out of the way, nailing it to his cross" (Col. 2:14).
>
> Now here is the point. If a great God who loves justice is yet so merciful as to forgive you, *what right have you* to fail to forgive yourself? Ephesians 4:32 says we are to forgive each other because God has forgiven us. Can it help but follow: It is just as necessary to forgive yourself.[11]

In the Gospels we have the story of Jesus healing the man sick of the palsy; that is, he was a paralytic and had to be carried by four men.

Jesus said to the man, "Son, be of good cheer, thy sins are forgiven thee." [12]

Jesus was saying, "Take heart, have courage." He instilled in the heart of that man a joy beyond description. To anyone reading this book who may be struggling with guilt and the inability to forgive yourself, He offered the paralytic healing, forgiveness, and good cheer all in one package. That's an offer that's valid today for you. He liberated him. Forgiveness liberates.

Often at the beginning of a political convention there will be the keynote speech. Jesus keynoted His ministry of liberation when He stood up in the synagogue at the outset of His public work and read the Scriptures. The Book of Isaiah was handed to him, and he opened it to the place where it says:

> The Spirit of the Lord is upon me; he has appointed me to preach Good News to the poor; he has sent me to announce that captives shall be released and the blind shall see, that the downtrodden shall be freed from their oppressors, and that God is ready to give blessings to all who come to him.[13]

In three brief years of His public ministry following that, He showed what was meant by those words. He demonstrated what it means to be free from the guilt and power of sin. No one needs to carry around a burden of gnawing accusations that scream you killed your son, you consented to the death of your wife, you are an adulterer. There is liberation through God's forgiveness and healing, and that healing takes place the moment you apply it to yourself and forgive yourself. Just that quickly the transaction is complete.

Notice the man who *was* a paralytic—no more will he have to be carried around by others, no more will he have to rely upon crutches or lie upon a stretcher while others gaze upon him in his pathetic condition. I can almost see him. Can't you? The Bible says he jumped up and left! When Jesus said to him, "Be of good cheer," I can imagine that the look of fear was immediately erased from his face.

Christ wants us to exhibit a cheerful countenance also. Our faith and trust in Him should produce that look on our faces that lets others know we have been the recipient of something very special—God's love and forgiveness. The touch of Jesus that heals!

God is willing to make the best of us, but we have to be willing to give him the worst of us! That young paralytic man left praising and glorifying God. But what if he had held back? Would there have been such healing?

Forgiveness of self is like the surgeon's scalpel that can open and remove the pus from a wound. Forgiveness of self enables the ugly, hurting emotional wounds you have suffered to be freed of that which festers, poisons, and prevents healing. Give up your guilt to the Great Physician just as you would happily give up a gangrenous arm if it meant the rest of you would be spared. Whatever it is that is placing you under a sentence of self-condemnation, give it up to Jesus, name it for whatever it is, hand it over to Him.

He wants it. He is your burden-bearer. He came specifically to help people like you. He wants your guilt. See it as Jesus sees it—undesirable, damaging, and threatening. You represent the body of Christ, you are important to Him, and He knows you cannot represent Him well if you are unwilling to let Him cancel out your inability to forgive yourself without any mental reservations.

Do you like nursing your guilty conscience, licking your wounds, feeling sorry for yourself? In a very real sense this is what you are doing so long as you fail to forgive yourself.

Dr. Maxwell Maltz, famous plastic surgeon and author of many successful books, best known for his amazing volume *Psycho-Cybernetics,* says this regarding the need to forgive one's self: "Not only do we incur emotional wounds from others, most of us inflict them upon ourselves."

We beat ourselves over the head with self-condemnation, remorse, and regret. We beat ourselves down with self-doubt. We cut ourselves up with excessive guilt.

Remorse and regret are attempts to live in the past emotionally. Excessive guilt is an attempt to make right *in the past* something we did wrong or thought of as wrong in the past.

Emotions are used correctly and appropriately when they help us to respond or react appropriately to some reality in the present environment. Since we cannot live in the past, we cannot appropriately react emotionally to the past. The past can be simply written off, closed, forgotten, insofar as our emotional reactions are concerned. We do not need to take an "emotional position" one way or the other regarding detours that might have taken us off course in the past. The important thing is our present direction and our present goal.

We need to recognize our own errors as mistakes. Otherwise we could not correct our course. "Steering" or "guidance" would be impossible. But it is futile and fatal to hate or condemn ourselves for our mistakes.[14]

Dr. Maltz goes on to say that in contemplating our own mistakes (or those of others) it is helpful and realistic to think of them in terms of what we *did* or *did not do,* rather than in terms of what the mistakes *made us.* Remember, he says, that "you" make mistakes, but mistakes don't make "you"—anything. To prevent or remove emotional hurts, we must be willing to live creatively, to be a *little* vulnerable. To trust, to love, to open ourselves to emotional communication with other people, he says, is to run the risk of being hurt.[15]

There is nothing more destructive than self-flagellation, which is what we are doing when we cannot forgive ourselves. We are all human and will make mistakes, say and do things that at times can leave us hating ourselves. But this is part of being a normal human being. Discover and accept your humanity and remember that God must have thought a lot about our humanness. After all, He chose to come Himself in the flesh!

A wounded self-love will in the end destroy itself. "By contrast, a self-respecting person . . . recalls his accomplishments, relives the happy moments stored in his memory and hopefully reflects on his optimistic future."[16] The result can be a strengthened, healthy self-love that is able to forgive one's self.

To be forgiven by God is to experience healing and deliverance. It triggers a wonderful liberation from a defeated past and the beginning of a fresh, new start in life. The same can happen when you forgive yourself. You have nothing to lose and everything to gain. Forgiveness is not *a way*; it is *the way*. It is the *only way* for the Lord or for us to deal with a sinful, guilty past.

9

How to Be More Prodigal than the *Prodigal*

You see them every day—long-haired, bearded, sandaled, loaded down with all sorts of paraphernalia including ditty bags, bedrolls, knapsacks, tents, sometimes even accompanied by a mongrel dog—these restless, wandering nomads. They have become knights of the roads, have-thumb-will-travel nomads hustling rides on freeways and highways.

At other times you may see them—combed, respectable-looking, expressionless. These, too, are restless, unhappy, bored, disillusioned youth. Yes, they live at home, but the alienation is just as great as though they were thumbing their way from where they are to who knows where! Alienated from parents and most often also alienated from God.

Whether at home or hitchhiking their way across country, you can be reasonably sure in a great many instances that the alienation has at its roots misunderstandings and that there is unforgiveness involved.

I think of Tom (not his real name). He was angry! He'd had it with his parents. He'd been accused of something that was absolutely not his fault, but his protestations of innocence were ignored. His parents simply would not believe him; they did not trust him. Even when he'd proved his innocence, they kept harping at him, nit-picking, making life miserable, to say the least.

He couldn't forgive them for their treatment of him. Accordingly, he decided to have his revenge by taking off. He'd split for California.

He, too, became a knight of the road. But the farther he got away from home, the heavier the backpack seemed to get. Yet he was lightening it every day—eating up the canned goods and food he'd taken from his mother's well-stocked cupboard.

Nights were the hardest. He felt lucky if he found a pad to crash; at other times he unrolled his sleeping bag and slept on the ground in a park or someplace where the police wouldn't find him and order him to move on.

One day he looked at himself in a gas station mirror. Unshaven, dirty scraggly hair, greasy jeans, soiled shirt. He knew he was a mess. And he could hardly tolerate the odor of his own body. *You're a bummer,* he thought to himself.

He tried analyzing his feelings as he shuffled along a lonely stretch of highway. Why had he left home? He tried answering that question as he grooved, rapped, and grassed his way to California. But deep down inside he knew the truth—he'd made a mistake.

The terrible. gnawing feelings inside him grew. The consequences of running away from home were catching up with him. He was sick of it all. Lonely, hurt, depressed. That was the day he stopped beside a phone booth. *Should I call home and ask their forgiveness?* He pondered the thought. It didn't take long to make up his mind. End of a wayward journey!

It had been an angry, foolish, rash, spur-of-the-moment act on Tom's part to leave home. It cost him agonizing, foot-weary, heartbreakingly lonely hours of travel, sleepless nights, a hungry stomach much of the time, and no satisfaction what-soever. It could have cost him his life.

But like the biblical prodigal, there is a time of coming to one's senses. How much better to spare oneself the misery and heartache, as well as one's loved ones the grief and concern, and not do rash, spur-of-the-moment things.

What is it that causes young people as well as adults to do things they only end up regretting later? In the case of hitch-hiking young people a California juvenile officer says in almost every case the problem can be traced to lack of communication. Perhaps it would be more accurate to say bad communication. There may even be excessive vocalization—too many hasty, ill-considered words. Or there may be the silent treatment, which in many respects is noisier than a barrage of words. Again, there may be irritating action—slamming of doors, rattling of pans (by one's wife, for instance), kicking the pet cat, turning up the hi-fi unnecessarily loud, throwing down one's school books, or storming angrily out of the house. Bad communication may show itself in a flushed face, flashing eyes, a rasping and abrasive tone of voice. Allowed to go unresolved, barriers build up. No one is willing to say, "I'm sorry, forgive me."

Tom is representative of thousands of young people who disregard parental and other adult advice and opt for learning the hard way. Some never learn and pay with their lives instead. You can read about them in newspapers and magazines, and hear about them on radio and TV news. They are playing a dangerous game of truth or consequences, but they soon learn it's not a fun game.

Even though some of us adults may never have tried the running-away-from-home bit and hitchhiking across the country, from the vantage point of experience and maturity, we can look back upon valuable lessons learned, and thus we try to spare our children mistakes we made. In other ways even now, however, we may be playing an equally dangerous game of letting self-will take over. One writer, relating this to the subject of forgiveness (or lack of it), says we are often guilty of playing self-protective games of false forgiving.[1] By whatever name you call it, or how you look upon it, it is phony forgiveness.

Rebellion against parental and adult hypocrisy accounts for much of the dissatisfaction and unhappiness so evident in many young people. They see through our phony games. Tom looked beyond his present predicament to the end result. What he saw he realized was not for him. He envisioned a life of emptiness. He may have been free from parental pressure, but what good was freedom when there was nothing to really live for and no one with whom to share? Freedom?

Michael Esses, a tantrum-throwing, rebellious Orthodox Jewish rabbi who is now a charismatic Christian minister and teacher, who rebelled to the point of near suicide and ran away from his wife and family before his electrifying personal confrontation with the Lord, explained what that kind of freedom spelled out to him:

> Free for what? To be lonely? To have no one who cares whether I live or die? Free to become a bitter old man? As I sat in my motel room in Miami the enormity of what I had done began to dawn on me. I was like a man who was slowly beginning to wake from a terrible nightmare. Even though it was my own creation, it was still a nightmare.
>
> The face of my little boy, Donnie, as he stood on the curb waving bye-bye to his daddy, swam in front of my eyes. My God, what had I done? Betty had stood beside me through all these years. How on earth could I justify what I'd done to her now? I knew there must be complete chaos at home. Here I was again, with my life in a million pieces, and as usual, it was I who had smashed it to the floor. Thus began a night filled with regret, remorse, and then wonder whether there was anything I could say or do to compensate my family for the failure I had been as a husband and father.[2]

But Michael Esses did come to himself just as young Tom did. It was a telephone call on the part of each of these asking for forgiveness that changed the direction of their lives. And then it was the exercise of a willingness to forgive and forget by Tom's parents and Michael's wife that bridged the communications gap and not only effected a glorious reconciliation for everyone involved, but even more important brought a return to a right relationship with God the Father.

We could well call such individuals contemporary prodigal sons. Is there a parallel? Consider the well-known biblical account of the prodigal son. Does a diet of corn husks stolen from a pigpen appeal to you? How about eating out of back alley trash cans? It wasn't exactly what the prodigal had in mind either when he left home to go his merry way! Contemporary prodigals are only repeating the sorry story.

The biblical story of the prodigal son shows the scope of God's mercy and forgiveness in a way in which the average individual can readily identify, for we have all been wayward prodigals to some degree, at one or more points in our life. The parable beautifully relates the forgiving fatherhood of God. The more we see and come to understand this readiness of God to forgive, the more anxious we should be to demonstrate such gracious forgiveness.

When the biblical prodigal decided to leave home, he did so with his father's knowledge, having first demanded of him his rightful share of the inheritance. "Give me my share of the estate now . . . !" were his words. He might at least have put a little more in his mouth and have had the courtesy to say, "Please give to me. . . ."

He yearned for liberty falsely so called, as he soon learned. It became the greatest form of slavery he had ever known. He was unappreciative of his father, distrustful and dissatisfied with his lot in life. His desire for independence almost became his ruination before his father showed willingness to forgive and take him back.

Our God is a giving Father, long-suffering, kind, and merciful. The prodigal's father exemplified our Lord's great love. What a compassionate Heavenly Father He is! The character and consequences of sin are clearly shown in the prodigal's actions. Self-will, sketched here in such appalling colors, always brings with it ultimate disillusionment, suffering, slavery, and despair. These are inevitable consequences of indulging in action contrary to God's will.

The prodigal son packed all his belongings and took a trip to a distant land, leaving behind his father and an older brother. In his new environment he wasted all his money on parties and prostitutes. About the time the money was gone a great famine swept over the land, and he began to starve. He persuaded a local farmer to hire him to feed his pigs, but he became so hungry that even the pods he was feeding the swine looked good to him. And no one gave him anything.[3]

What a commentary that is on human nature—no one gave him anything. No one took pity on him. No one offered to relieve him in his desperate plight. The same people who so gladly helped him spend all his money in riotous living were now nowhere to be found. Willful waste brings woeful want.

The common misery of sinners, those who flaunt the Father's grace, is that they throw away their own mercies, the favor of God, their interest in Christ, the admonitions of the conscience. Not only was the prodigal living in a land of famine, but what was even worse, there was a famine in his soul—the inner man. Not only was he hungry and longing for food, but there was no satisfaction for his soul. A sinful state is a state that cannot expect relief from any person. No mere man can feed and nourish one who is starving for sustenance that God alone can supply.

The prodigal, the Bible tells us, finally came to his senses. His sin had not been mere folly; it had been madness and frenzy. We destroy ourselves when we allow ourselves to get into the grip of Satan, our adversary. But when the prodigal was brought to the last extremity and realized the extent of his desperate need, he did not give way to despair. He was saved from that.

I dare to believe he had a praying father who was interceding on his behalf, a loving father who was pleading God's intervention and promising the Heavenly Father that he, as an earthly father, would forgive his erring child. This father had never ceased to love his son and prayed, hoped, and yearned for his eventual return. In fact, the Bible gives reason to believe he spent time looking for the prodigal's return.

Consideration of the sad state we are in is the first step toward conversion. The prodigal considered and turned. He compared his past and present circumstances. He had to see for himself his miserable state; just so, we must see ourselves for what we are if we are to be driven to our knees in repentance and confession seeking the mercy and forgiving love of God the Father.

The Bible records that the prodigal said to himself: "At home even the hired men have food enough and to spare, and here I am, dying of hunger! I will go home to my father and say, 'Father, I have sinned against both heaven and you, and am no longer worthy of being called your son. Please take me on as a hired man.' " [4]

Let the backslider take heart—the individual who feels he has so violated God's will that there is no possible restoration and forgiveness for him. It makes no difference to what degree of bondage to sin we have fallen, there is grace enough for the vilest of backsliders who will but cry out to their Father for mercy and forgiveness.

There are two necessary conditions to receive God's forgiveness and full pardon—confession and turning from sin. Notice the prodigal as he realizes that his offense has been not only against a loving earthly parent but against God. "I have sinned against heaven," he asserts. [5]

Yes, sin is an affront to the God of heaven. We forfeit the

glories and joys of heaven when we sin and refuse to admit it. It is said that the malignity of sin aims high; it is against heaven. The daring sinner is said to have set his mouth against the heavens, according to the writer of Psalms. How we need to learn that what is shot against the heavens will but return upon the head of him who shoots it. It literally boomerangs.[6]

The prodigal's admission of guilt is an acknowledgment that he knows he has forfeited all the privileges of sonship. God is pleased when we are willing to humble ourselves before Him like this. Genuine sorrow for sin reaches the Father heart of God. In this parable Jesus shows us the matchless love of God to every repentant soul as we look at the prodigal's father and see forgiveness in action.

Did the father say, "Why didn't you stay with your prostitutes and pigs"? Was there condemnation? Rebuke? An I'll-give-him-just-what-he's-got-coming attitude? No. There was nothing but love and affection, for the father had been waiting for the return of this prodigal. The son returned slowly, under a burden of shame, guilt, and fear; but the tender father, who had been patiently and prayerfully watching, saw him coming even while he was a long distance away. The father was filled with loving pity and ran and embraced and kissed his son.[7] Just so, God, because of Jesus, is ready, free, and willing to receive that individual who is sorry for his sins and returns to Him.

The father's actions in embracing and kissing his son demonstrated forgiveness even before he spoke a word. There are times when actions speak louder than words. It was the son who uttered the first words, living up to what he had told himself when he first came to his senses. "Father, I have sinned . . ." but he was interrupted by his parent who began calling out directions to the servants: "Quick! Bring the finest robe in the house and put it on him. And a jeweled ring for his finger; and shoes! And kill the calf we have in the fattening pen. We must celebrate with a feast, for this son of mine was dead and has returned to life. He was lost and is found." [8]

The son would have been grateful if his father had just allowed him to go to work as one of his hired servants, but here was his father calling for beautiful clothes not just to clothe him, but to adorn him. He was in rags and shoeless. No longer would he walk barefoot looking and acting as a beggar. His father even went a step further in calling for a ring. The ring was a seal of power, a constant memorial of his father's kindness and forgiveness.

How rich this parable is in showing us God's forgiveness. No wonder Jesus used it to teach, among other things, that God bestows blessings abundantly beyond our petitions and prayers. We may be fearful, lacking hope, fully aware of our shortcomings and knowing that we deserve rejection, yet God as our Father not only receives us but receives us with respect. It is a picture of complete restoration. It provides assurance that God takes us to Himself, into closest fellowship as sons and heirs. He gives us the righteousness of Christ as a robe, the garment of salvation. Isaiah, the prophet, depicted it so beautifully when he declared, "Let me tell you how happy God has made me! For he has clothed me with garments of salvation and draped about me the robe of righteousness. I am like a bridegroom in his wedding suit or a bride with her jewels." [9]

There is something else here that we must not fail to notice. The Apostle Paul tells us that the Christian's armor—that which we "put on" spiritually to enable us to withstand the evil one's assaults and which aids us as we go out to do battle for the Lord—includes "having feet shod with the preparation of the gospel of peace." [10] Isaiah says, "How beautiful upon the mountains are the feet of those who bring the happy news of peace and salvation, the news that the God of Israel reigns." [11]

The prodigal's father's action in calling for shoes for his son's feet signifies that God, when he receives true penitents into his favor, will use them for the convincing and converting of others. Sadly, there are those in the Christian world today who would strip restored prodigals of not only their robes of righteousness but also their shoes!

David, when pardoned, taught transgressors the ways of God. And Peter, when he finally came to himself, not only strengthened his brothers and sisters already in Christ but went out and converted thousands through the power of the Holy Spirit that came upon him.

It is difficult enough to walk in "the Way" with shoes that are able to speed us on the way, but how difficult we make it for those whom we should be helping when we refuse forgiveness. We not only take away their shoes but then throw broken glass, tacks, and raw splinters in their way. May God have mercy on us who are more prodigal than *the* prodigal.

The prodigal came home ravenously hungry. His father not only fed him but feasted him. The fatted calf, which had been given special food, reserved for some very special occasion, was brought out, killed, and prepared. Only the best would do for this child who was once dead to his father but now was alive again, who was once lost and now was found.

The return of prodigals ought to bring great rejoicing to God's people. We should take note of events that affect God in heaven and cause Him and His angels to rejoice. The saints are to rejoice in God's goodness.[12] Just as the prodigal's father feasted him and welcomed him back into the family, so we must not withhold forgiveness nor the things that will nourish and strengthen those who may have offended, or in some way departed from what *we* feel is the acceptable way of doing things.

There is another side to this story that cannot remain without comment, and it involves the elder son—a hardworking fellow. When he returned home from the fields where he had labored for long hours, he heard music coming from the house. He asked one of the servants what was going on.

"Your brother is back," he was told, "and your father has killed the calf we were fattening and has prepared a great feast to celebrate his coming home again unharmed." [13]

One would think this son would have broken into a run, shouting with joy, calling out his brother's name. But no, he was angry and wouldn't even go in the house! [14] He begrudged his brother his father's kindness, forgiveness, and love. He himself showed lovelessness and disgusting pride. He could not think in terms of what this meant to his father, nor how wonderful it was to have his brother back, safe and sound, restored to the family and reconciled to God. He was offended to the highest degree, and he betrayed his selfishness and self-righteousness as he boasted of his own virtue and obedience, pointing out to his father, "All these years I've worked hard for you and never once refused to do a single thing you told me to; and in all that time you never gave me even one young goat for a feast with my friends. Yet when this son of yours comes back after spending your money on prostitutes, you celebrate by killing the finest calf we have on the place." [15]

The elder brother showed the pharisaical attitude, surely not the spirit of Christ. He depicts souls out of fellowship with God just as much as the prodigal son before he came to himself. There is no real joy in God's service for such as these. Their religion is merely a matter of unwilling obedience and loveless faithfulness to their own private interpretation of God's laws without regard to God's mercy. They know not the meaning of true forgiveness because they haven't experienced it for themselves. They may have a fairly clean slate, believing they have preserved their reputation, but they are sour, ill humored, harsh, and censorious.

The elder brother's forgiveness couldn't stretch far enough to include his once fallen but now restored brother. The message of this parable comes through loud and clear: We are to receive those whom God has received; we are to admit them into favor, friendship, and fellowship. The elder brother was arrogant; he called his brother "your son" as he spoke of him to his father. "This son of yours," he said with contempt. He would not own him as his own brother.

The Bible tells us that God does not mark iniquities when they are confessed. The parable shows us up for what we are when *we* paint others with the blackest colors begrudging them the Father's kindness and forgiveness. The elder brother envied his brother the grace of both his father and God.

We should not forget that the Apostle Paul, before his conversion, had been a prodigal. Look at the havoc he was attempting to make of the early church. Then let us examine the other apostles who could rightly be considered his elder brothers. They had been faithfully serving Christ even while Paul, then called Saul, was persecuting them. Did they envy Paul's conversion experience, his visions, and later the way God chose to use him? Certainly their attitude was the reverse of the prodigal's elder brother, showing us clearly the need to receive and help restore those who may have fallen away from the Lord, but who do come to themselves and return.

The father's answer to the elder son stands alone in beauty and truth. "Look, dear son," his father said to him, "you and I are very close, and everything I have is yours. But it is right to celebrate. For he is your brother; and he was dead and has come back to life! He was lost and is found!" [16]

The Scriptures do not tell us whether the elder brother yielded to his father's entreaty. All we can do is hope that he recovered his temper and that he, too, came to himself.

But Jesus was delivering a parable to the Pharisees. Did *they* catch all of the rich meaning meant for their own good? Jesus was saying to them that He came to seek and to save the lost, which included the hated Gentiles. He came to forgive men their sins, and He expected the same exercise of loving, forgiving grace from them. Would they continue to criticize and envy the repentant sinner? I believe Jesus was saying to all of us, *Forgive as I forgive, and live together as the family of Christ. You are all my sons and my daughters.*

10

How Do You Make a Lover out of a Hater?

You can't sit at a lunch counter in a restaurant or rub shoulders with your fellowman in various areas of life without coming away with the strong feeling that everyone is facing problems of one kind or another. No one is immune from situational difficulties or emotional disturbances. As I listen in on beauty parlor conversations, for instance, I see the need for everyone to possess the good grace that says, "Yes, I forgive you."

One day, as I sat writing this book the doorbell rang. It was Larry, the termite inspector (we'd just sold our home). People are always curious about my occupation as a writer, a fact that cannot be denied when they encounter my desk and the surrounding area! The sign on my desk bravely proclaims: *A clean desk is the sign of a sick mind.* (That little sign does more by way of explanation for me than any words or excuses I might try to devise!)

When he learned the subject of this book—forgiveness— Larry sat down in a chair with a "Now, that's something I can tell you about. Have *I* ever had to do a lot of forgiving in *my* lifetime!" (He looked too young to have had *that* many experiences. Object Lesson Number One: Forgiveness is an exercise we begin early in life and never cease practicing.)

"Can you imagine spending four days in jail because you spanked your son when he ran out in the street and almost got run over?"

I glanced at the young father sitting opposite me. He was the personification of bright young fatherhood, dark-haired, slender in build, his ruddy features bright and animated. Earlier conversation had revealed his love of reading and the fact that he was very knowledgeable.

"You mean you actually were thrown into jail because you spanked your little boy after he ran out into the road and was almost run down by a passing motorist?" I rephrased the question, wanting to make certain I'd heard him correctly.

"That's right," he replied. "My nosy neighbor, who didn't have anything better to do with her time than peer through her curtains looking for ways to devise trouble in the neighborhood, phoned the police after I paddled my son's behind, scolded him, and sent him into the house."

"And you ended up behind bars four days in the local jail?" I was incredulous.

"Yep! And lost my job to boot."

"You mean you were fired from your job because—"

"Because of all the newspaper publicity." He took the words out of my mouth.

"What did you say to the judge when you were being interrogated about this?" I questioned.

" 'Your Honor' "—he dramatized it grandly—" 'did your father ever spank you when you were little and did something wrong?' I did some interrogating on my own," he volunteered as I laughed. "The judge said he'd been spanked aplenty. 'Well, then, Your Honor, it shouldn't be too difficult for you to understand the situation I found myself in the other day. You see, my little son wandered out onto the busy street in front of our house when he'd been warned never to do this. I love my little boy and want to see him grow to manhood. I had to teach him a lesson he wouldn't soon forget, nor did I want him to repeat his mistake. Sir, I spanked my son in the proper place. And I spanked him so he'd remember it the next time he was tempted.

" 'Now, Your Honor, if you let me out of this jail, I'm going home to be a good father, same as I was before I got put in this place. And if one of my children does something wrong, something they've been told they must not do, I'm going to paddle them. If that's the wrong way to discipline children, then you'd just better lock me up again. The Good Book tells me to "train up a child in the way he should go, and when he's old he won't depart from it," and it also says, "Spare the rod and spoil the child." I know it tells me not to withhold correction from my children and even says something about using the rod. I used my hand and corrected him. I intend to keep on disciplining my children the way I believe is best. I'm doing it because I love them.' "

The outcome of that true story is that the judge was, as I suspected, very impressed. Larry's son had not been harmed in any way, no bruises had been found on his little behind, and Larry was released.

"The judge asked me who was responsible for turning me in," Larry stated. "I had to point to my neighbor. The judge told her to stop meddling in other people's business and to get busy and involved in some worthwhile activity in the community."

"We were talking about forgiveness . . ." I reminded him with a smile.

"Ah, yes," he laughed. "Forgiveness. *Forgiveness in action,* you said. It took a lot of grace," he reminisced. I could see the wheels turning. He had told me it had happened a number of years ago. "I was able to do it—I really did forgive her. I felt sorry for her. She got nothing but kindness from me. 'Vengeance is mine, saith the Lord, I will repay.' " He knew his Bible and wasn't afraid to quote it. "I learned long ago there's only one way to treat those who mistreat you—love 'em to death. They can't stand it; they can't figure that kind of treatment out. It really bugs them."

But that wasn't all. He'd had another brush with the law that could have left him bitter. When I commented to that effect, he said, "Hey, no way. Who gets hurt when you let bitterness take over? *Me. You.* Not the other guy."

It seems that he'd come home from work one evening to find a citation on the table. "My wife and kids were romping in the front yard of our home with the dog. Guess they were really having a good time. This policeman came along and wrote out a citation because she didn't have the dog on a leash. Imagine that! In my own front yard yet! Ended up costing me twenty-five dollars.

"I couldn't take time off work to fight it. Would have ended up costing me more—lawyer, time off, et cetera. So we paid the money and I just say I don't like the system, the whole economics of the structure. But what's a man going to do?" He shrugged his shoulders.

"Forgive?" I looked at him—a questioning look with raised eyebrows.

He laughed. "That's the answer. He nodded his head affirmatively. "Tell your readers it's *the only answer.* Sometimes you have to even forgive the law."

Yes, and then there are those times when we have to forgive and seek forgiveness from co-workers. Like my friend Warren who was caught in a dilemma at the aircraft plant where he worked in our community. He tells it like this:

"Two other Christians and myself got together at lunch time for Bible study. We prayed that the Lord would open a door for us to have a growing Christian fellowship at work. One day in the plant newssheet we noticed a little footnote: 'Anyone interested in Bible study, please contact. . . .' So I called the name given. He was an enthusiastic, effervescent Christian. That began our Bible Fellowship, and we had a wonderful time for the first three months.

"Then my two friends and I got transferred to the main building where the others in that fellowship were already located. I have a Bible school background, and so the fellows asked if I'd help teach. Well, the man who'd put the notice in the newssheet was the teacher, and he took offense at that. I was really caught in the middle. But under pressure from the others I did do a lot of the teaching. It was a blessing, and the group grew.

"Eventually, Nick dropped out of the fellowship, and I went to see him about it, feeling as I did that according to the Bible this is what I must do. Actually, I have never seen such rancor, even in a nonbeliever. You talk about roots of bitterness—this was the best illustration I have ever seen of what can happen when a person is unforgiving.

"I spoke to him about the need for being reconciled according to Matthew 5:21–25. He called me names, said I was sneaky, subversive, and an egocentric maniac. It was a real blow. It took four years before he was willing to admit that he'd been nurturing this grudge. During all this time he'd been away from the Lord, he admitted. Ephesians 4:32 says to be kind one to another, tenderhearted, forgiving one another even as God for Christ's sake hath forgiven you. But it prefaces that by stating, 'Let all bitterness, and wrath, and anger, and clamour, and evil speaking, be put away from you, with all malice.'

"I believe that the root of bitterness springs from malice. Sometimes I think we are successful at putting away our anger about a given situation, but we overlook the necessity, as the Bible emphasizes, to be sure that any lingering malice is banished. Malice is evil intent, a desire to harm others. Believe me, I learned a lot from that experience."

Incidentally, at his place of work Warren is called "the

disciple of love," as he seeks actively to stir up others in the love of Christ.

Earlier in the fourth chapter of Ephesians (4:20) we discover a clue as to why we, even as Christians, may fail in our relationships with others. The Apostle Paul says, "You have not so learned Christ." The meaning is, "You have not learned Christianity—the things Christ taught and the rules of life prescribed by Him."

The Amplified Bible says,

> Assuming that you have really heard Him and been taught by Him, as all Truth is in Jesus—embodied and personified in Him: Strip yourselves of your former nature—put off and discard your old unrenewed self—which characterized your previous manner of life . . . and be constantly renewed in the spirit of your mind—having a fresh mental and spiritual attitude; And put on the new nature [the regenerate self] created in God's image [Godlike] in true righteousness and holiness. . . .[1]

We are to learn Christ! Christ is not a book, a lesson, a way, a trade. He is a Life. In Jesus God expressed Himself. Until we come to Christ, we are "alienated from the life of God." [2] It is in Jesus' life that we see embodied the true standards of living that we are to seek to imitate.[3] Paul was writing to those who were once enthralled by pagan vices and vanities, but until we learn Christ and "put on" the virtues that belong to the new life of Christian holiness, we are no different from them.

There is a new life concept that comes into focus when we accept Christ. The guiding instrument in the mind, that faculty of feeling, understanding, and the will, that instrument of the spirit, that Paul says must be brought into subjection while constantly changing for the better. Clothe yourself with this new nature, he says.[4] This new nature, this ideal humanity, that we learn from Christ's own life is to then express right conduct toward our fellowmen.

The precepts of the Apostle Paul are not out of date. He gives us a comprehensive list of non-Christian vices and Christian virtues, presenting a series of moral contrasts. Falsehood is contrasted with truth, anger with forgiveness, theft with doing good, corrupt speech with edifying words, bitterness with love, uncleanness with purity, drunken folly with spiritual fervor.[5]

In this chapter we have been speaking of malice, which must have no place in the Christian's life. Every kind of ill will, malignity, rooted anger and spite must go. The way to accomplish this is through the supreme Christian motive of love. We find our model and impelling motive in the forgiveness of God, "even as God also in Christ forgave you." The God Who forgives like that was Himself manifest in Christ.

Kindness and forgiveness are the specific spheres in which the example of God in Christ is to be followed. In Ephesians 5 Paul continues his argument, reasoning that the motive for living and walking in love can be best illustrated in the self-sacrificing pattern of Jesus. The whole course and conduct of our lives should reflect the fact that we are "imitators of God." Phillips translates it like this: "As children copy their fathers, you, as God's children, are to copy him. Live your lives in love—the same sort of love which Christ gives us and which he perfectly expressed when he gave himself up for us in sacrifice to God." [6]

As parents we hope our children will imitate us in all things that are inherently good. Just so, the character we bear as God's children places us under a supreme obligation to resemble Him, especially in His love and goodness, in His mercy and readiness to forgive.

In the practical outworking of our lives, what does this do to and for us? It enables Larry, a termite inspector, to forgive his neighbor who had him thrown in jail for spanking his son and even makes it possible for him to forgive the law for imposing an unreasonable fine on him. It finally brings a

11

Paul's Strategy in Dealing with Hostility

"When I get to heaven, first thing I'm going to do is ask Jesus what he wrote in the dust on the ground!"

She sat on the couch in my living room, a fragile pink appearing doll in her pale pink and white long dress, her hair scooped up on top of her head, which she shook now with vehemence. Somehow her comment, uttered with such hostility, seemed out of place coming from this delicate creature. But I knew some of the background which prompted the outburst, and I could understand.

Penny was a victim of people forming judgments about her without any basis of known facts. She suffered from a severe neurosis for which she was receiving specialized help. She herself was the first to admit that she had problems and needed help. Her very honesty and openness made her especially vulnerable. But there was a lack of sympathetic understanding of her situation on the part of Christian friends— people who made no attempt to accept her even though they could not understand her various behavior patterns. Penny's sensitivity made her aware that she was the subject of their uncontrolled tongues.

She was fortunate, however, to have a husband who was patient and long-suffering. He loved her very deeply and spared no effort to give her the help she needed. That night, sitting on the couch in my living room, after she had made her comment, Bob [her husband], sitting opposite her, smiled indulgently as if to say, "I've heard this from her before," which, in fact, he had.

Those of us who heard Penny's comment, however, did understand. We truly loved her and accepted her. We loved her for the past hurts which had caused her such pain, and we loved her now for the Herculean efforts she was making to regain her footing. It wasn't easy. The long-buried hostility would surface now and then and had to be dealt with.

You may have said it yourself at one time or another, or surely you have heard it said by someone else—this comment, "When I get to heaven, I'm going to ask Jesus . . ." and then follows what often proves to be a revealing statement giving indication of a person's inner hurt.

I'm strongly inclined to believe, however, that the many questions that plague us here and that we think we're going to ask Jesus about the first opportunity we get when we arrive in heaven, will be wiped out by the sheer beauty of His presence and the joys that await us there.

The Bible tells us, "Eye hath not seen, nor ear heard, neither have entered into the heart of man, the things which God hath prepared for them that love him." [1] We have no idea what a blessed prospect awaits us in that prepared place the Bible calls heaven! Here on earth we put up with misery, heartache, unpleasantness, defeat, problems, hurts, humiliations, misunderstandings. But the frustrations and sorrows of this life will vanish when we stand in the presence of God and our eyes drink in His glory and the greatness of His love.

There is a quality missing in the experience of many Christians, which is not as it should be. "They are so busy enduring their failure that they have no time to enjoy their faith. The one thing the world needs to see today is a quality of joy that cannot be obtained by human logic." [2]

Imagine writing a letter from prison and stating, "Rejoice in the Lord always: and again I say, Rejoice." [3] Paul did it in the book that has been called the most joyous book in the Bible, his letter to the Philippians. He uses the words "joy" and "rejoice" seventeen times in four short chapters.

Paul was no extra-special, priviliged sanctified saint, but he had a confidence and courage that transcended the dismal experiences that were often his lot. "I know whom I have believed" [4] was his powerful testimony. The joy Paul experienced and wrote about is available for every believer today. God plays no favorites, and Paul was no exception.

Did Paul know something that you and I don't know that enabled him to speak with such confidence and positive certainty? Paul didn't have any private line to heaven that gave him additional insight you and I can't possess. But Paul did have a truly adequate concept of God's forgiveness which so filled him that his every waking moment was lived in the consciousness of the greatness of God's generosity.

God's love was a power that had invaded Paul's life from the moment God first struck him down on his way to Damascus to persecute the Christians. In Acts 9, at the outset of the chapter, we read of Saul, uttering threats and intentions of slaughter against the followers of Christ called Christians. God spoke to him even while in his garments he carried warrants to arrest every believer in Damascus.[5] He was bent on persecuting and killing the Christians, yet this voice said to him, "Paul, Paul! Why are you persecuting *me?*"

When Paul asked who was speaking, the voice replied, "I am Jesus, the one you are persecuting." [6] God actually threw Paul, then called Saul, to the ground as he leveled the charge against him that he was persecuting Him. Before Saul could become a great saint, one to be mightily used by God, he had to be made to see himself as a terrible transgressor rebelling and sinning against Christ.

Paul thought he was persecuting only a company of poor, weak, silly people who were an offense to the Pharisees and the Jewish religion. God set Paul straight and in effect said, *you are persecuting Me the Lord of glory, the God of heaven and earth.*

A really humbling conviction of sin is necessary if one, like Paul, is to carry with him a conscious reality of God's forgiveness. This is what Paul may have known to a greater degree than some of us so that it was possible for him to say so emphatically, "I know whom I have believed."

The recognition that he was actually persecuting Christ came quickly to him. He lay there convicted and condemned. He who had been a blasphemer of Christ's name now addresses Him as Lord.[7] The experience on the Damascus road blinded him, but three days later he not only received his sight back but was filled with the Holy Spirit.

Paul had three days to reflect with terror about his past and to understand how close he had come to sinning even further against God if he had not been stopped in his tracks. God did not abandon him those three days, but sent Ananias to care for him and to speak to him about what had happened.

Paul was to become a standard-bearer for Christ; he was destined to suffer great things for that one Who bore the cross for him and suffered the agonies that would secure our forgiveness and access to heaven. Paul did have an extraordinary call, and for it he was given extraordinary qualifications. God revealed Himself to him in this dramatic way so that he would go out with great power, full of Christ Himself, the Spirit constraining him to preach, proving that Jesus was the Christ, the anointed of God, the true Messiah, the one Who forgives and reconciles us to God.

God's love for us, however, is the same as it was for Paul.

He doesn't deal with us all in the same way. Paul's experience was unique, unmatched. But *you* are unique to God also. Paul recognized that God's forgiveness and salvation began at the cross and then His love stretched to the ultimate in dimension when it included him. That same recognition can be the experience of every child of God. Forgiveness is the access we have to the Father's heart. It is the access we have, therefore, to heaven.

To my troubled friend, struggling with feelings of hostility, to you—whoever you are—and to myself, I would point to the quality of faith Paul exhibited and to his joy and suggest that we examine closely the claims this man makes. He has earned the right to speak so boldly.

Paul catalogs for us the catastrophes that befell him in 2 Corinthians 11:23–33. If ever anyone had cause to feel hostile or want to question God when he gets to heaven about the why behind his suffering, it should be Paul. He wrote:

> I have worked harder, been put in jail oftener, been whipped times without number, and faced death again and again and again. Five different times the Jews gave me their terrible thirty-nine lashes. Three times I was beaten with rods. Once I was stoned. Three times I was shipwrecked. Once I was in the open sea all night and the whole next day. I have traveled many weary miles and have been often in great danger from flooded rivers, and from robbers, and from my own people, the Jews, as well as from the hands of the Gentiles. I have faced grave dangers from mobs in the cities and from death in the deserts and in the stormy seas and from men who claim to be brothers in Christ but are not. I have lived with weariness and pain and sleepless nights. Often I have been hungry and thirsty and have gone without food; often I have shivered with cold, without enough clothing to keep me warm.
>
> Then, besides all this, I have the constant worry of how the churches are getting along: Who makes a mistake and I do not feel his sadness? Who falls without my longing to

help him? Who is spiritually hurt without my fury rising
against the one who hurt him?

But if I must brag, I would rather brag about the things
that show how weak I am. God, the Father of our Lord
Jesus Christ, who is to be praised forever and ever, knows
I tell the truth. . . .

Yes, Paul knew what it meant to be mistreated by those
who claimed to be brothers in Christ. But he submerged his
hostility by saturating himself with thoughts of the forgiveness
and love of Christ. It worked every time. Paul qualifies to
speak from bitter experiences. His word to us is that we, too,
can have strength for all things in Christ Who empowers us
—makes us ready for anything and equal to anything (and
anyone) through Him Who infuses inner strength into us.
Paul says we can be self-sufficient in Christ's sufficiency.[8]

I have a strong suspicion that when my fragile friend, who
really does possess great inner strength and does so love her
Lord, gets to heaven, she will radiate His joy—which she has
been radiating here on earth—and will lift her pretty little face
to the face of that one Who forgave and yet forgives her, and
she'll say, "Thank You, Jesus, for Your love and forgiveness."

12

Understanding Is Involved in Forgiveness

Jesus was *always* the perfect gentleman. I could weep—thankful tears—every time I read or hear Hebrews 4:15, which says, "We have not an high priest which cannot be touched with the feeling of our infirmities. . . ."

The Amplified Bible expresses it so tenderly: "We do not have a High Priest Who is unable to understand *and* sympathize *and* have a fellow feeling with our weaknesses *and* infirmities *and* liability to the assaults of temptation, but One Who has been tempted in every respect as we are, yet without sinning."

And Phillips says it like this: "For we have no superhuman High Priest to whom our weaknesses are unintelligible—he himself has shared fully in all our experience of temptation, except that he never sinned."

What comfort that gives to those of us who have weaknesses and who know what it is to be assaulted by temptation! We all stand soiled, accused before God, until we have accepted and experienced Christ's forgiveness. We are no worse,

but surely no better, than the woman dragged before Jesus—
this pitiful creature who had been caught in the act of adultery.
You may not like being compared to one such as she—you
may indeed not be guilty of that particular sin—but we can
never get away from *the fact* that our Lord said impure
thoughts are sinful as well as impure deeds.

The story can be found in John 8:1–11. Once again we
encounter the right-righteous Pharisees. The employment of
the means they used this time to trap Jesus is a pitiful reflec-
tion upon their character and motives.

This time they come dragging the woman caught in adultery. Their aim was to place Jesus in a dilemma, and they
didn't care what means it took to do it.

It is not difficult to imagine this woman's shame and em-
barrassment. She stood wretched and guilty, before Jesus, the
crowd, and her accusers. The writer Charles L. Allen says
that possibly she was standing there unclothed since women
were stoned while naked, and more than likely her garments
had already been ripped off. The humiliation must have been
very great. Her accusers had made up their minds to stone
her to death, since according to the law of Moses this was
what she deserved.[1]

There are those, sad to say, among the ranks of Christen-
dom who seem to enjoy another's shame. But this was surely
not true of Jesus. In no way would He add to her humiliation
and agony. Jesus crouches down, He does not look at her,[2]
and in that loving act He stands taller than any person in
that crowd.

As Jesus bent down, His finger scrawled out a message in
the dirt. Much speculation has arisen through the intervening
centuries over the actual content of Jesus' message. Whatever it was, it and the words He uttered—"Let him who is
without sin among you be the first to throw a stone at her"[3]
—had the desired effect.

Christ did not act contrary to either the ecclesiastical or

the civil law of His time. He lifted the whole incident out of the sphere of mere legal technicalities into the realm of moral realities. It was a beautiful gesture. He and He alone is qualified to judge rightfully all men; by this action and utterance He silenced, convicted, and condemned His enemies and the woman's. It was as if He said, "Look, you self-appointed executors of divine justice, if you want to take the place of God, then make certain your lives are just as pure."

His penetrating gaze went right through those men. There wasn't one individual among them who morally qualified to do what the group had set out to do. In another book I make the observation that these men did not dare take away with their hands a life that they had already tried to take away with their tongues.[4]

We have such limited knowledge, such limited understanding of the heart and life of another. None of us can claim the right to point an accusing finger at another.

> There is always a reason behind every action. . . . "To know all is to forgive all," is an ancient proverb housing a half-truth. The truth in it? Understanding underlies forgiveness! But that's only half the truth.
>
> Because your most perfect understanding of any other person might only breed contempt, not forgiveness. Any human understanding of another human is tainted with our own evil. None of us is good enough to be entrusted with complete knowledge about another.
>
> And that's impossible to begin with. You can't come to know another person bit by bit and cell by cell. That's not the purpose of understanding at all. The real purpose is only to help us see the difference between what the sinner *did* and what the sinner *is!* Yes, he *did* wrong, but there *is* more to him than that single misdeed.
>
> Don't try to understand the other person. Try instead to be understanding.[5]

David Augsburger summarizes this by stating that any attempt to understand someone else leads to an exercise in hypocritical superiority and is inescapably judgmental. When we start impugning motives and prejudging another's attitudes and actions, stereotyping them into cubbyholes of our own construction, classifying and permafreezing them into neat categories, we are "playing God."

Understanding is involved in forgiveness. It's described by the Apostle Paul in his letter to the Christians at Colossians in this fashion: "Accept life, and be most patient and tolerant with one another, always ready to forgive if you have a difference with anyone. Forgive as freely as the Lord has forgiven you. And, above everything else, be truly loving, for love is the golden chain of all the virtues." [6]

This, of course, explains why Jesus did not condemn the woman caught in adultery. If she was standing there trembling and naked, as some commentators believe, then I would imagine Jesus' first act was to cover her nakedness. He would, no doubt, have turned to the crowd and asked someone to drape something around her. The writer of Psalms expresses it so well when he says, "Blessed is he whose transgression is forgiven, whose sin is covered." [7] The idea is that forgiveness of our sins is something that needs to be continually exercised upon us. David, who wrote that, knew what it was to experience God's forgiveness (more about David in Chapter 14).

"Forgiveness is the cloak for our naked, sinful souls." [8] He covers us with His love. He covered her with that love. As man, the Perfect God-Man, He bore about Him like a beautiful golden chain this virtue of love, as the Apostle Paul described it. Another writer friend, Eugenia Price, believes the woman taken in adultery sinned because of hunger. She was hungry for love. Her sin was the sin of twisted love.

The scribes and priests sinned, too, but their sin was the sin of self-righteousness and greed (what other sins lay covered, unexposed, we do not know). Genie Price believes the woman caught in this act did not run away (she could have after her accusers left) because she was seeking love, and in Jesus she recognized love personified. She waited, because standing before Him, she saw not only the sin in her own life but the hope for her in His forgiveness. And this is what forgiveness does for an individual—it opens up the door of hope. "It has been said that the most redeemable person alive is the one who has sinned seeking love." [9]

Jesus sent this woman on her way uncondemned. He said to her, "I do not condemn you. Go on your way, and from now on sin no more." [10]

His favor to her and to all whom He forgives of sins that are past is a strong argument to do as He commands, "Go and sin no more." The Apostle Paul gives a lengthy treatise on this in Romans 6, and it would pay the reader to examine that passage closely.

Once again we have the lesson: "Judge not, that ye be not judged. For with what judgment ye judge, ye shall be judged: and with what measure ye mete, it shall be measured to you." [11]

Jesus did not mean that we should not condemn that which we know to be wrong, but if we are to communicate spiritual truth and show forth His love, we cannot engage in the spirit of faultfinding. If we are really interested in helping others overcome the environmental or internal factors that are tempting them and plunging them into sin, we will not drag them and their sinfulness into the gaze of the public eye. Rather, we will endeavor to help them overcome their besetting sin, their problems and defects in character.

It is God's prerogative to try the heart; we do wrong when we try to step into His throne. Jesus is saying that God will not show mercy in His judgment of us if we are showing no mercy to the reputation of others. The Bible says with reason that the merciful shall find mercy. We show great reverence to the Word and love of God and our fellowmen when we consciously strive to refrain from rash judgment.

> Why do you criticize and pass judgment on your brother?
> Or you, why do you look down upon or despise your
> brother? For we shall all stand before the judgment seat
> of God. For it is written, As I live, says the Lord, every
> knee shall bow to Me, and every tongue shall confess to
> God—that is, acknowledge Him to His honor and to His
> praise.
>
> And so each of us shall give an account of himself—give
> an answer in reference to judgment—to God. Then let us
> no more criticize and blame and pass judgment on one an-
> other, but rather decide and endeavor never to put a stum-
> bling block or an obstacle or a hindrance in the way of a
> brother.[12]

Paul is reminding us that the court of heaven is the only
proper court for trial! Contentions and differences do exist
among Christians, but Paul is here stating that Christ is to
be the arbitrator at the great day of judgment; meanwhile,
there is more than enough for us to do to keep ourselves in
good account.

James has something to say on this also. What an important subject it is as we thread our way through the Bible making these significant discoveries:

> My brethren, do not speak evil about or accuse one an-
> other. He that maligns a brother or judges his brother is
> maligning and criticizing the Law and judging the Law.
> But if you judge the Law, you are not a practicer of the
> Law but a censor and judge of it.
>
> One only is the Lawgiver and Judge—the One Who has
> the absolute power of life and death—Who is able to save
> and to destroy. But you, who are you that you presume to
> pass judgment on your neighbor? [13]

James, who wrote this, was called James the Just. It is believed that in this passage he was calling the people's attention

to the Old Testament law of Moses that said, "Thou shalt not go up and down as a tale-bearer among thy people." [14]

Thus, our lips must be governed by the law of kindness, as well as truth and justice, always holding out forgiveness and understanding.

13

The Devil Wears a Familiar Face

"I am deeply a part of the problem for which Christ died." [1] Leave it to writer-friend Keith Miller to make that kind of an observation about himself. I greatly appreciate what he has done for the thinking Christian's life in jolting us into the necessity of being honest with ourselves. In his first book, *Taste of New Wine*, he knocked the props out from under thousands of us by calling for a new kind of honesty that recognizes and faces squarely the nature and extent of our deceitfulness with God, with each other, and with ourselves.

Just whom do we think we are fooling, anyway? Certainly not God, for He sees us as we really are. When Samuel was sent by the Lord to seek out a king to take Saul's place, he was sent to the home of the sheepherder Jesse. (We would be inclined to object, "Lord, what an unlikely place to find someone suitable to be a king!") How much we need to learn what God so plainly taught Samuel, the prophet, that day.

As Samuel scanned Jesse's sons, he looked at one called Eliab and thought, "Surely the Lord's anointed is before Him."

But the Lord said to Samuel, "Do not look at his appearance or at the height of his stature, because I have rejected him; for God sees not as man sees, for man looks at the outward appearance, but the Lord looks at the heart."[2]

Frequently, we judge by the sight of the eyes, but God does not. Isaiah in speaking of the root of Jesse, which root was to come from the family of David in the line of lineage, states that He (Christ) will not judge by what His eyes see.[3]

We need to exercise our spiritual senses if we are to look at ourselves, first of all, as we really are. To do this requires honesty and courage. We must stop deluding ourselves. We must level with God. He wants us to. The Apostle Paul wrote, "Examine yourselves whether you are in the faith."[4] Paul is saying, "Take off your spiritual blinders and test yourself before you test others. If there is something counterfeit in you, acknowledge it to God." Paul's counsel is that God will not reject you when you put yourself on trial.

The writer of Proverbs assures us of this also: "He that covereth his sins shall not prosper, but whoso confesseth and forsaketh them shall have mercy."[5]

In this matter of judging others and failing to forgive others, as we look at ourselves, we may find some long-buried matters that require straightening out.

The closer a person gets to God, the more honest he will be about himself, and therefore the more grace he experiences. Grace is only grace when it is not deserved, when it is not worked for. And this is precisely the point! Our honesty before God which brings us to Jesus Christ is the only "lever" that will release the flow of God's love. The expression of our need opens our lives to his power. So the sick go to the doctor and outcasts come to Christ to enter the kingdom. So the humble are in heaven. and life's failures become the salt of the earth.

Is it strange? You would expect the salt of the earth to be the accomplished, sophisticated leaders of men, the finest, the cultured, the highest ethically. To the contrary, the salt of the earth are the humble, the suffering, the empty, the spiritually poverty-stricken—in other words, sinners anonymous. This is the truth of Christianity which need not be camouflaged under superficial performances. . . .

When we forget these basic truths given to us by Jesus Christ, we only continue to steer ourselves into our present dilemma. The only way out is honesty with ourselves and one another and God. Perhaps we have to begin with God, for as we become honest with Him without faking, we learn from Him to be honest with ourselves. Nothing prevents God from loving us. He will not turn his back on us in spite of our waywardness. He has demonstrated his unchangeable love once and for all in the life and death of his only Son. We cannot help but marvel all our lives long that such grace is freely given. This is the greatness of the good news, where all sham ends. The misery of a sinner and the mercy of God! [6]

The first recognition that we have not been practicing the kind of forgiveness the Bible speaks of, and to which this book is directed, may come with stunning impact. Our recollections of past unforgiving actions, attitudes, and words may make us very miserable.

At this point the devil may rear his familiar face with remembrance of misdeeds others have done against us. He may remind us of the unkind words, the gossip, and the slander others have said about us. The faces of family members, friends—those closest and dearest to us (if not now, at one time in the dismal past, which we've been trying to keep buried)—may rise up to haunt and even taunt us. We may mentally draw up a long list of grievances and slam shut the door to future dealings with certain people.

The devil wears a familiar face. He may come disguised as a friend—one you considered to be a friend at one time, but no more, not after what he or she did to you and said about you. Unforgiveness. We practice it subtly whether or not we consciously realize or admit it.

The devil wears a familiar face. He may come disguised as your husband or wife or ex-husband or ex-wife. The hurts and insults you took from him or her are a thing of the past, but now, as you look honestly at yourself, you find a host of unforgiven things.

The devil wears a familiar face. Does he look like an unforgiven son or daughter? An aunt, uncle, father, or mother? What of your neighbor or business acquaintance who cheated you ruthlessly, a brother, a sister, or an in-law? Something in you cries out, "Injustice has been done. They've lied about me. They stole from me. They've maligned my good name. They've kept me from getting that tremendous job. . . ." Yes, some of our scars are deep, and just looking at them again causes them to hurt once more.

You may even be so disillusioned by what someone has done to you, particularly if they say they are a Christian, that you've even stopped fellowshiping with them and no longer attend church with any regularity and possibly not at all. Have you said, "I've forgiven them, but I just don't want anything more to do with them"—or with Christianity or the church or whatever they represent?

That, my dear reader friend, is not forgiveness. And it is you who stands to be hurt and harmed the most. It is emotionally, physically, spiritually, and mentally destructive. It is keeping you from experiencing God's love and forgiveness, and it may keep you from heaven unless you come to this moment of truth before God and yourself by admitting that you've been harboring unforgiveness in your heart (which God sees) and are willing to make an honest confession.

Yes, the devil wears a familiar face. He may even look like you. And if you continue to give him a foothold in your life, refusing to do battle with him in this matter of forgiving others, then the reality of what I talk about in the last chapter of this book applies to you. You may have a very respectable righteous look about you, you may attend church twice on

Sunday and once on Wednesday night, and if the Ladies Aid meets monthly or twice monthly, you'll be there also. But God knows you are wearing a mask. He wants to relieve you of that false pretense once and for all. He yearns for you to understand the truths of His Word relating to this need to forgive others and to treat others with justice and love.

There is hope and help. God knew that we would all fall short of His glory. He did something about it. He sent His Son. You've read about Him in this book. You may even claim to know Him in a very personal way. If you do, then you know Jesus went all the way to the cross.

> Jesus Christ himself . . . suffered the scandalous, public death of a sinner in our stead. He was not ashamed to be crucified for us as an evildoer. It is nothing else but our fellowship with Jesus Christ that leads us to the ignominious dying that comes in confession, in order that we may in truth share in his Cross. The Cross of Jesus Christ destroys all pride.[7]

"Confession? Wait just a moment." Are you saying something like that? Do you not like the implications of that word? "Okay, so I've been guilty of not forgiving certain people. If I confess it to Christ, does that get me off the hook? Does that make everything all right? Can I be sure of getting into heaven if I honestly admit to the Lord that I've not been on the up-and-up with forgiveness of those who've wronged me?"

David, the man after God's own heart, learned the hard way what it is to live with guilt and unconfessed sin, unforgiving attitudes against another. It was like a rotting of his bones. Let him tell you what happens, however, when guilt like this has been forgiven.

> What happiness for those whose guilt has been forgiven! What joys when sins are covered over! What relief for those who have *confessed their sins and God has cleared their record.*

There was a time when I wouldn't admit what a sinner I was. But my dishonesty made me miserable and filled my days with frustration. All day and all night your hand was heavy on me. My strength evaporated like water on a sunny day until I finally admitted all my sins to you and stopped trying to hide them. I said to myself, "I will confess them to the Lord." And you forgave me! All my guilt is gone.

Now I say that each believer should confess his sins to God when he is aware of them, while there is time to be forgiven. Judgment will not touch him if he does.[8]

Confession before God is therefore necessary. But there is also the possibility that you may need to make restitution and confession to those from whom you have been withholding forgiveness. This is where we back off, where we want to part company, where we want to say, "So long, it's been nice knowing you, but that's not for me."

"Where right relationships have been ruptured by sin, we sometimes need to show repentance through restitutions. To God we cannot make restitutions, we can only offer our worship. But for sins against men, restitution can and must be made." So writes John Stott in *Confess Your Sins.*[9]

Stott believes that we confess our sins in three ways. There is secret confession, made to God because they are secret sins. ("Our iniquities, our secret heart and its sins [which we would so like to conceal even from ourselves] You have set in the revealing light of Your countenance," writes the Psalmist.[10] These are sins committed against God only.) Then there are private confessions, made to individuals against whom we have sinned. Finally, there is public confession, because some sins are committed against a group or congregation and must be confessed publicly.

In the final analysis all sins are actually committed against God, and we are answerable for them before Him. But when our misdeeds and unforgiving attitudes are against man also, there are those who believe one's spiritual development is impaired when confession is not made and forgiveness sought. It is true that to have a right relationship with God, we must also have a right relationship with others. To what extent this means actively seeking out the offended ones and making confession is a matter that must be left with the reader.

The Book of James says, "Confess your sins to one another, and pray for one another." [11] The Amplified Bible enlarges on that idea like this: "Confess to one another therefore your faults—your slips, your false steps, your offenses, your sins; and pray (also) for one another, that you may be healed and restored—to a spiritual tone of mind and heart."

Dietrich Bonhoeffer says:

> Confession in the presence of a brother is the profoundest kind of humiliation. It hurts, it cuts a man down, it is a dreadful blow to pride. To stand there before a brother as a sinner is an ignominy that is almost unbearable. In the confession of concrete sins the old man dies a painful, shameful death before the eyes of a brother. . . . [12]

Are there instances, however, when it is best not to make open confession to someone else? If it will be more redemptive and loving to the other person involved, the answer to that is yes. Do not seek healing for yourself at the expense of another's suffering which may result.

How does this work, for instance, where a husband or a wife has been unfaithful and the mate does not know? Dr. Harold J. Sala writes:

> Of course, if a mate knows, you must face the matter and seek forgiveness, but if he or she does not know, and you are quite certain will never know, it is an entirely different matter. In some cases, I believe that confession to an innocent husband or wife who otherwise would never know of a mate's failure, only brings greater personal grief and distress.

Why hurt an innocent person and destroy the confidence he
or she feels? [13]

Dr. Sala recommends that after confession has been made
directly to God, confession to a trusted pastor is in order, but
he advises (and there are many trained counselors, psychol-
ogists, and pastors who would agree with this) that you spare
your mate unless you can find peace of mind no other way.

I believe a word of caution is in order about confessing to
one's most intimate friends. Do not impose upon others your
burden of guilt if it is not necessary to your own spiritual
welfare. Remember, God is bigger than our problems and
wants us to cast them upon Him, for He careth for us.[14] God
is our source of forgiveness and release from guilt.

David Augsburger believes that confession should only be
as public as the commission of the act. Only those directly
involved should be told in your confession. Confession should
not be so intimate, so revealing, so painful, that it will wound
or scar the person to whom it is made. Careless, thoughtless
confession to a close friend, a lover, or a spouse may bring
you release, but it will transfer the painful burden to another.[15]

Absolute honesty before God is the most crucial confession
of all and leads to His forgiveness. Keith Miller was absolutely
correct when he said, "I am deeply a part of the problem for
which Christ died."

14

Qualifications for a Man after God's Own Heart

Forgiveness, like love, kindness, and other virtues, is something one does, not just something one talks about. Actually, forgiveness is really the outworking of love, and to be true forgiveness, it must spring from the heart. Jesus said it: "A good man out of the good treasure of the heart bringeth forth good things; and an evil man out of the evil treasure bringeth forth evil things." [1]

The Amplified Bible makes it especially plain: "The good man from his inner good treasure flings forth good things, and the evil man out of his inner evil storehouse flings forth evil things." Preceding verses talk about one's words and speaking. Jesus always made His message to His listeners very easy to understand. He used common examples with which they were familiar. This time, in talking once again to the Pharisees, He used the illustration of a tree, reminding them that a tree is identified by its fruit. A tree from a select variety produces good fruit; poor varieties don't. [2] Then, in strong, startling words, Jesus says:

You brood of snakes! How could evil men like you speak what is good and right? For a man's heart determines his speech. An evil-hearted man is filled with venom, and his speech reveals it. And I tell you this, that you must give account on Judgment Day for every idle word you speak. Your words now reflect your fate then: either you will be justified by them or you will be condemned." [3]

The people looked upon the Pharisees as a generation of saints, but Jesus calls them a generation of vipers. Never forget that it was a viper, an ugly snake, that first brought enmity between God and our original parents, Adam and Eve. Jesus' words were heard by His disciples that day—a warning to them (and us) so that we might know what sort of men we live among.

The heart is like a tree. Trees have roots. If it's a good tree, its roots go down deep, and the tree produces beautiful good fruit. If there is a root of bitterness in our lives springing from malice and unforgiving attitudes, then it is impossible for us to speak and bring forth words that will show we are men and women after God's own heart.

The heart may also be likened to a fountain. Words are the streams that issue from the fountain. Solomon, considered by many to be the wisest man who ever lived, said:

Like a muddied fountain and a polluted spring is a righteous man who yields, falls down and compromises his integrity before the wicked. . . . The words of a whisperer or slanderer are as dainty morsels or words of sport (to some, but to others are as deadly wounds), and they go down into the innermost parts of the body (or of the victim's nature). Burning lips (uttering insincere words of love) and a wicked heart are like an earthen vessel covered with the scum thrown off from molten silver (making it appear to be solid silver). He who hates, pretends with his lips, but stores up deceit within him. [4]

Elsewhere Jesus said, "Evil words come from an evil heart,

and defile the man who says them. For from the heart come evil thoughts, murder, adultery, fornication, theft, lying and slander. These are what defile. . . ." [5]

How we need to remember, even as Solomon said in Proverbs, that death and life are in the power of the tongue.[6] The Pharisees, to whom Jesus was speaking, were supposed to be familiar with Solomon's teachings. Jesus was only repeating what they supposedly already knew when he reminded them that by their words they would be justified and acquitted, and by their words they would be condemned and sentenced.[7]

When the heart is right, we do things right; but when the heart is wrong, there are so many things we do wrong. A heart that is right cannot withhold forgiveness.

> Forgiving is cooperating with God in the promotion of goodwill in His kingdom. . . . Forgiveness is one of the ways we can keep in tune with the Lord in His great redemptive program. Forgiveness is the great liberation God extends to all who commit their ways to Christ. Forgiving others liberates our own hearts from enslaving emotions and attitudes. Forgiving others is one of the good things we do for ourselves.[8]

What is it that makes a person a candidate to be called a man after God's own heart? We have already seen what God thinks of a heart that is not producing good things. The logical place to look to see what it is that God seeks in a man's heart is the man about whom it was said that "he was a man after God's own heart." That man is David, whose life we have already looked at to some degree in previous chapters.

The Apostle Paul, in reciting some of the history of the nation of Israel in the synagogue at Antioch, mentioned David by describing him as the man God chose to replace King Saul, whom He (God) removed. Paul said God chose David, a man after His own heart, *because David would obey Him.* So we see that obedience is a requisite if a person is to know God's favor.

There are sixty-two chapters in the Bible devoted to David's life. His is the fullest biography in Scripture. His was a spectacular rise from shepherd boy to the throne of Israel. Those quiet years in the home of Jesse, his father, in Bethlehem stand in vivid contrast to the years spent in the splendor of the palace; yet those years trained him for the high destiny to which God called him.

Solitude can teach us much if we are willing to be taught. While tending his flock of sheep, David was learning lessons of patience and courage. Here, too, out on those quiet hills he could sing and play on his harp, and it is thought that many of his Psalms were composed while he was there tending sheep. It was not without reason that he was called the sweet singer of Israel. He was magnificently gifted with musical skills.

David's father and Samuel, the prophet, were astounded that God should choose sixteen-year-old David rather than his more impressive older brothers. But it only serves to emphasize even more the scriptural principle that God is more concerned with internal attributes than with physical appearance and appeal. From the moment that Samuel anointed David, the Bible tells us he was Spirit-filled.[9]

What would such an experience do to most young people? David remained unaffected by what occurred. His ego was not inflated. Rather, the anointing imparted a new purpose and sense of divine destiny to his young life; then, as in later life, David displayed amazing self-discipline. Often in his Psalms David speaks of "waiting patiently for the Lord." God had set him apart, and so David would not waste his time in impatient wondering or mistrusting God's plan and promise to him.

David knew what it was to meditate and pray. That is why

through succeeding generations the Psalms have remained un-excelled for beauty in meditative purposes.

It was David's epic encounter with the giant Goliath that made him a national hero. The details of this famous combat are well known; what is less generally known and recognized is that David's victory was essentially a triumph of faith. In what is considered the "roll call of faith" chapter in the Bible, Hebrews 11, David is mentioned. It was because these people, including David, trusted God that they won their battles.

David appeared before his adversary in a plain shepherd's coat. There was no breastplate of metal. In his hand he carried his sling and five smooth stones he had casually picked up from the brook.[10] When Goliath saw David approach, he sneered in contempt at this nice little red-cheeked boy![11]

David depended upon God for success. David shouted to Goliath: "You come to me with a sword and a spear, but I come to you in the name of the Lord of the armies of heaven and of Israel—the very God Whom you have defied. Today the Lord will conquer you. . . . The whole world will know that there is a God in Israel! And Israel will learn that the Lord does not depend on weapons to fulfill His plans—He works without regard to human means!"[12] David was absolutely fearless because he was strong in his faith. He sought no honor for himself but devoted the praise and glory of it all to God. Is it any wonder that God, Who sees the end from the beginning, would call David a man after His own heart?

But while David now was the idol of his nation, this episode made King Saul very jealous, and from that moment on David lived in constant danger, which ended only when Saul died. Four attempts on David's life were made by the king. When the tide of the king's displeasure ran against him, David conducted himself with great wisdom, and the Lord was continually with him.[13]

David's life was a kaleidoscope of experiences which touched the deep wells of human emotion at all points. It has been rightly said that no other Bible character experienced so many swift changes of fortune as David. He walked a rugged and lonely road for nine years while Saul pursued him. On two different occasions David could very easily have killed Saul, but David demonstrated loyalty to the king. Even more important, he would not do anything that would frustrate God's purpose for himself and the nation he had been chosen to serve.

To live a life worthy of the potential with which God has endowed us is difficult under any circumstances. For David it was even more difficult than for most. David knew that God understands the language of the heart, so that often in the Psalms we read of him crying unto the Lord with his voice, and we always read, "And the Lord heard me." Over and over again we also read. "And the Lord sustained me."

David's troubles always brought him to his knees. In spite of the circumstances surrounding his life that were often most grievous and difficult, he could still say, "Thou hast put gladness in my heart." [14] True joy like this is joy that God gives. It is solid, substantial. Jesus, when He knew He would be leaving His disciples, said, "I am leaving you with a gift— peace of mind and heart! And the peace I give isn't fragile like the peace the world gives. So don't be troubled or afraid." [15]

Though David did not live on this side of the cross, he experienced that peace and abiding joy. What was the secret of this secure feeling that David evidenced? It was in staying close to God, committing all his affairs to God, and contentedly leaving the issues with him. David kept himself in the love of God through obedience and seeking forgiveness when he knew he had strayed. This the man after God's own heart will always do.

David experienced the rejection of his favorite son whom he had unwisely indulged and who later usurped his kingdom for a period of time. He knew what it was to be betrayed by his friends. His own nation rejected him and forced him into exile. He understood fatigue, hazards, uncertainties. Through all of this, however, he practiced forgiveness of his enemies long before it was enjoined by the Lord.

All of this is not to say that David was a perfect man. It is meant to show the reader that it is possible to live a life that habitually and consciously practices forgiveness. David did have faults and did experience failure. The Bible always paints men in true colors with no distortion. David's life also vividly demonstrates that godly men and women may fall grievously. David was fully aware that God cannot tolerate sin, that it must be confessed and expiated. Psalm 5 is but one of many Psalms that reveal David's awareness that the Lord abhors and rejects deceitful men: "For You are not a God Who has pleasure in wickedness, neither will the evil (man) so much as dwell (temporarily) even with You. Boasters can have no standing in Your sight. You abhor all evildoers. You will destroy those who speak lies." [16]

David's experience in yielding to the passions of the flesh and committing adultery with the beautiful Bath-sheba, the wife of Uriah, one of his warriors at the battlefront, was a dark stain on his life. David paid for this sin with great guilt and grief. The child born to Bath-sheba died.

That sin left indelible marks on his home and family. There is no such thing as a simple sin. Sin is always complicated. David lost the smile of God for a period of time. It has been said that the dove of peace flew from his heart. Even his throne lost its stability, and his testimony before his people and the surrounding countries was tarnished.

> The bright spot in the sordid affair was that the enormity of his sin was matched by the depth of his repentance. How men react *after* they have been sifted by Satan is a revelation of their true character. For a whole year, and maybe longer, David remained in stubborn unwillingness to confess his sin.[17]

It was the prophet Nathan whom God used to bring David to his senses (see 2 Samuel 12). When the prophet presented a hypothetical case that produced swift anger in David, we see David immediately confessing, "I have sinned against the Lord." David saw his sin in its true light. At that moment Psalm 51 had its birth:

O loving and kind God, have mercy. Have pity upon me and take away the awful stain of my transgressions. Oh, wash me, cleanse me from this guilt. Let me be pure again. For I admit my shameful deed—it haunts me day and night. It is against you and you alone I sinned, and did this terrible thing. You saw it all, and your sentence against me is just. But I was born a sinner, yes, from the moment my mother conceived me. You deserve honesty from the heart; yes, utter sincerity and truthfulness. Oh, give me this wisdom. Sprinkle me with the cleansing blood and I shall be clean again.

Wash me and I shall be whiter than snow. And after you have punished me, give me back my joy again. Don't keep looking at my sins—erase them from your sight. Create in me a new, clean heart, O God, filled with clean thoughts and right desires. Don't toss me aside, banished forever from your presence. Don't take your Holy Spirit from me. Restore to me again the joy of your salvation, and make me willing to obey you. Then I will teach your ways to other sinners, and they—guilty like me—will repent and return to you. Don't sentence me to death. O my God, you alone can rescue me. Then I will sing of your forgiveness, for my lips will be unsealed—oh, how I will praise you.

You don't want penance; if you did, how gladly I would do it! You aren't interested in offerings burned before you on the altar. It is a broken spirit you want—remorse and penitence. A broken and contrite heart, O God, you will not ignore.

And Lord, don't punish Israel for my sins—help your people and protect Jerusalem. And when my heart is right, then you will rejoice in the good that I do and in the bullocks I bring to sacrifice upon your altar.[18]

Nathan assured David of God's forgiveness. "Yes, (you have sinned against the Lord) but the Lord has forgiven you, and you won't die for this sin. But you have given great opportunity to the enemies of the Lord to despise and blaspheme him. . . ." [19] We see here the results of disobeying God. The Apostle Paul warns of this when he says, "You dishonor God by breaking His laws. No wonder the Scriptures say that the world speaks evil of God because of you." [20] How we need to beware that we are giving occasion to those outside of Christ to point to us and say, "If that's Christianity, I don't want anything to do with it!" We must not furnish the enemies of God with anything that brings reproach and blasphemes.

The nature of God's forgiveness is that we do not come under condemnation. Contrary to what some would teach, our sins do not have to mean our everlasting ruin when we confess and forsake them. Great sinners do not need to despair of finding mercy with God if they truly repent. We see this exemplified in the life of David.

David sinned another time in numbering the people in Israel.[21] There are those who say David's greatest sin was not with Bath-sheba, but the occasion when seventy thousand people lost their lives. God was displeased with David's political arithmetic. This was a sin of pride, not passion, and it involved the whole nation of Israel in God's judgment. God had said in a promise to Abraham that his seed would be as innumerable as the dust of the earth; yet here was David making calculations with no orders from God to do it, nor was there any occasion to warrant it. It smacked of distrust of God's promise and was an affront to Him.

David was guilty of proud conceit and proud confidence in numbers and the strength associated with numerical superiority. God does not need formidable numbers to overpower enemies, nor a multitude with force. It is wrong to trust in the arm of flesh when our reliance should be in God only. It took nine months and twenty days for this census to be taken. It

involved a great deal of needless trouble and effort on the part
of many people and it was all so unnecessary. It was simply
David's vanity that was being satisfied.

The sin of pride robs God of His glory. And when the sin
of pride goes on unconfessed and forsaken, it can be spiritually
ruinous. Once again, however, David saw his mistake. The
realization came right on the heels of the difficult assignment
being completed. When his conscience was awakened, David
felt great pain. The Bible says "David's heart smote him after
he had numbered the people." Notice how quickly his conscience bothers him as he says to the Lord, "What I did was
very wrong. Please forgive this foolish wickedness of mine." [22]

Again, God did forgive. This time there was a just and
necessary correction to be administered for this sin. Of the
seven things that God hates, according to Proverbs 6:17, pride
is the first. David refers himself and his people to God's mercy,
"It is better to fall into the hands of the Lord (for His mercy
is great) than into the hands of men." [23]

For this sin God sent a great pestilence to the land and
70,000 men, who had all been in good health, were sick and
dead, in a matter of a few hours. God can so easily bring
down the proudest sinner. David was in great anguish and
pleaded with God, "I have sinned. I have done wickedly, but
these people, what have they done? Let your anger be only
against me and my family."

David is saying we must be quick to seek God's forgiveness
and then to accept whatever He gives as His mercy. Scripture
tells us that Jesus was led as a lamb to the slaughter. He, our
great Shepherd, was smitten for us, the sheep. I am sure
David would say it is better to be severe with one's self now
than to face God's judgment and condemnation later.

We wish that David's life had not included these episodes
—and there were others—that seem to stand as an indictment
against the man described as a man after God's own heart.
I believe, however, we would have to say that because he was

so human—capable of great emotion, no stranger to tears, who knew what it was to hunger for human love, prone to make mistakes—we can the more readily identify with him.

> He swung between extremes, but paradoxically evidenced an abiding stability. The oscillating needle always returned to its pole—God Himself. His ambitions were spiritual, not personal. His greatest concern was, in the main, the glory of God. Throughout his life there was a singular absence of carnal ambition, but a consuming desire to secure the glory of God. The key to David's life and achievements, marred though they were by failure, is found in *his inner attitude to God*. His defections were temporary, accidental rather than characteristic.[24]

If you would be called a man after God's own heart, it would pay you to become very familiar with the life of David. One important key to his nature is the strong element of gratitude that pervaded him. There was thankfulness for what God had accomplished in his life and for a God Who forgives. The man after God's own heart must know what it is to receive God's forgiveness, and then he must be willing to hold out that same forgiveness to others.

15

God's Perfection Calls for Forgiveness

I did not know my father. He died five months before I was born. But I always knew he must have been a wonderful man. I knew because Mama spoke of him with such love. I especially liked to hear her tell of the time he was hit on the cheek by someone, and then he turned to that person and said, "The Bible says if someone strikes you on one cheek, you are to turn to him the other also." Often Mama would tell the tale when I was angry and would come in from play, all mad, hot, and bothered. It never failed to subdue me. I would reason to myself: *If Daddy could do that, so can I.*

I knew, too, that it was biblical. We read the Bible three times a day in our family—morning, noon, and night. The Bible was kept on a small ledge under the table where we ate all our meals. Even when we were in school and would run home at noon for lunch, Mama would pull out the Bible and read. Frequently, we had the Bible with dessert when we were short on time. Mama would forgo dessert to read to us.

Reading the Bible at meals was a practice dating back

to Mama's days in her parental home. All devout Dutchmen read the Bible at the table. When we visited at my grandparents', you could count on Grandpa reading in his native tongue from his big Dutch Bible. I'm sure I fidgeted at home when Mama read, but I know I fidgeted something awful at Grandpa and Grandma's house. Later, after Grandma died and we went to live with Grandpa for a time, Mama did succeed in getting Grandpa to read from "the American Bible," as he put it.

Consciously and unconsciously, however, I was absorbing biblical truth. Mama also insisted on Bible memorization and learning the Catechism. I didn't much appreciate Saturday mornings as a child when I had to go to Catechism. But Mama knew what she was doing. "I have to be both mother and father," she would say with firmness in her voice, and you didn't disobey. If you did, there was always the ruler to be reckoned with. Mama believed in *not* sparing the rod, and she certainly did not spoil her children. She and Solomon agreed on child discipline!

There were other things Mama believed, and now, in my own more mature years, I can see how she put her biblical beliefs into action, including the admonitions about forgiveness. In the Iowa community where we lived my father had been a successful dairyman and had also raised champion purebred hogs. I'm certain he felt he was leaving my mother and her three children (one—me—as yet unborn) well protected and taken care of, but it is my understanding that after his death Mother was left with monstrous medical bills stemming from his long bout with terminal cancer. The details are unimportant; how it all happened I really do not know (nor do I care now to know), but Mother was wiped out financially.

The Bible admonishes Christians to care for the widowed and fatherless: "The Christian who is pure and without fault, from God the Father's point of view, is the one who takes care of orphans and widows." [1] That was written by James the Just. Paul the Apostle in writing to young Timothy said, "Let me remind you again that a widow's relatives must take care of her." [2]

Much space is devoted in this chapter of 1 Timothy to rules to be observed in caring for women who are left husbandless. Paul said kindness should begin at home by supporting needy parents or relatives. "Anyone who won't care for his own relatives when they need help, especially those living in his own family, has no right to say he is a Christian. Such a person is worse than the heathen." [3]

Jesus spoke strong words against those who dealt unscrupulously with widows. "Woe unto you," He said, "scribes and Pharisees, hypocrites! For ye devour widows' houses, and for a pretence make long prayer." [4]

Not only had my father on occasion willingly turned his cheek, but I saw my own mother turn hers. The blows she endured were strong. But she did endure them. Her faith was stronger, and in the end she was richer by far in other more important ways. She did not strike back. Retaliation was not in her nature. She kept her little family together, supporting them with the loving work of her hands. She was a professional seamstress. In addition, she kept a rooming house for young people from a nearby Christian academy.

Because she rented out every bedroom that could be spared, my sister and I shared Mother's bedroom. For years my sister slept in my father's hospital bed, and I slept with my mother. I have vivid recollections of seeing Mother nightly on her knees by the side of the bed. She knew what it was to pray for forgiveness for ill will, which would understandably spring up in her heart when she considered her lot in life.

The Old Testament allowed a law of retaliation, "an eye for an eye, a tooth for a tooth, hand for hand, foot for foot, burning for burning, wound for wound, stripe for stripe." [5] If a neighbor killed one of your beasts, you could go out and kill one of his. If your neighbor in some way blemished you, you were entitled to go right out and blemish him.[6] They did not need to show pity; it was literally a life for a life.[7]

When Jesus came along, it was, therefore, more than a little astonishing for those steeped in Jewish teaching and law to hear Him call for an entirely different way of life. The law of retaliation was to be abandoned and replaced by the law of love. We are not to take matters into our own hands but to leave everything in the hands of God. Jesus was calling for His followers to bear patiently the insults and injuries done to them by others. Listen to His words:

> The law of Moses says, "If a man gouges out another's eye, he must pay with his own eye. If a tooth gets knocked out, knock out the tooth of the one who did it." But I say: Don't resist violence! If you are slapped on one cheek turn the other, too. If you are ordered to court, and your shirt is taken from you, give your coat, too. If the military demand that you carry their gear for a mile, carry it two. Give to those who ask, and don't turn away from those who want to borrow.
>
> There is a saying, "Love your friends and hate your enemies." But I say: Love your *enemies!* Pray for those who *persecute* you! In that way you will be acting as true sons of your Father in heaven. For he gives his sunlight to both the evil and the good, and sends rain on the just and on the unjust, too.
>
> If you love only those who love you, what good is that? Even scoundrels do that much. If you are friendly only to your friends, how are you different from anyone else? Even the heathen do that. But you are to be perfect, even as your Father in heaven is perfect.[8]

Patiently endure. Conform to Christ's example. Do not insist upon privileges and your rights. Cheerfully accept whatever comes your way. We are to be peacemakers. Kindness is to be the rule and law of our life. We are to pray for others

—pray that God will forgive them for the wrongs they have committed against us. Do not expect the reward of Christians if you rise no higher in your virtue than that of publicans!

Some people cannot understand these words of Christ urging us to be perfect. In fact, many throw up their hands in despair and say, "I give up! I can't possibly attain to that."

What we fail to realize is the fact that God takes into account our inner motives. God reads the intent of your heart. My heart. Everyone's heart. We are to press toward perfection as we consciously aim to put into practice the teachings of the Bible. We may not always attain our goals, for we are human, finite, and fallible. Only God is infinite and infallible. He is divine perfection.

Paul speaks of this in Philippians 3. Here and elsewhere he expounds on the heavenly walk of earthly people. Not easy, Paul says! I struggle, too, he admits. I haven't attained, he reminds them:

> I don't mean to say I am perfect. I haven't learned all I should even yet, but I keep working toward that day when I will finally be all that Christ saved me for and wants me to be.
>
> No, dear brothers, I am still· not all I should be but I am bringing all my energies to bear on this one thing: Forgetting the past and looking forward to what lies ahead, I strain to reach the end of the race and receive the prize for which God is calling us up to heaven because of what Christ Jesus did for us.
>
> I hope all of you who are mature Christians will see eye-to-eye with me on these things. . . .[9]

Here is an "eye-to-eye" approach different from that to which the people of Paul's day were accustomed!

How does one attain to the perfection Jesus demanded? I believe it can be accomplished by looking at God's perfection and the perfect love of Christ, which sought the greatest and highest welfare of everyone by showing forgiveness in action. Christ was calling His followers to unclench their fists and learn the power of love.

It has been proved by the growth and survival of the early church that God blesses those who choose this perfect way of nonviolence and nonresistance as opposed to vicious persecution. How thankful we can be that those early Christians not only heard the Word and listened to the disciples, the Apostle Paul, James the Just, and others—but also responded with action.

Peter, who saw Christ insulted and struck by His enemies, remembered so well Jesus' reaction and faithfully recorded it. He shared it wherever he went preaching Christ and the crucifixion. It happened when Jesus was arraigned (so called) before those who had seized Him without cause. One of the officers struck Jesus with the palm of his hand.[10] Later, Peter said, "When he was insulted he offered no insult in return. When he suffered he made no threats of revenge. He simply committed his cause to the one who judges fairly."[11] Jesus did exactly what He advocated that His followers do.

I saw my mother overcome all the obstacles and hardships that came her way. I did not always understand or appreciate our situation in my growing-up years, but now I do understand. Mother was never overwhelmed by the events in our lives. Believe me, we had plenty of problems, but Mother knew that there were no problems in heaven, only plans that included her and the three children God had entrusted to her. She could trust Him to see us safely through. She would train her children in the way they should go, just as the writer of Proverbs admonished. And she would trust God to supply our needs. Not always were our wants met, but our needs were. Though we lived sparingly, she poured out the riches of God's love and mercy as she read to us from the Bible.

In my mother I saw forgiveness in action. She was not per-

fect and never claimed to be, but she did seek God's forgiveness for herself and others, and she freely extended it to others
also. In this and other ways she strived for perfection, and
you and I can, too.

16

Heaven May Be Smaller than You Think

The forgiveness of God through Christ cannot be claimed by those who are unwilling to forgive their own fellowmen. Yes, that is a very strong statement. It leads me to believe that heaven may not be as largely populated as one might suppose. Heaven may indeed be a small place in terms of those who are its occupants.

The Bible assures us that heaven is to be the eternal destiny of all those who are believers. Many references could be given, but it is an uninterrupted thread throughout the Bible. If one accepts the whole counsel of God, then one must take into account the teachings of Jesus on the subject of forgiveness in action, which is the theme of this book.

Have you ever stopped to think that you curse yourself every time you say the Lord's Prayer? You do if you are not practicing forgiveness. If you differ with this statement, your argument is with the Scriptures, for the teaching is there. Forgiveness of our fellowmen is essential if we are to secure

God's forgiveness and therefore the assurance of spending eternity in heaven with Him.

The Lord's Prayer is recorded in both Matthew's Gospel and the Gospel of Luke. The Phillips translation puts it like this:

> Forgive us what we owe to you, as we have also forgiven those who owe anything to us. . . . For if you forgive other people their failures, your Heavenly Father will also forgive you. But if you will not forgive other people, neither will your Heavenly Father forgive you your failures.[1]

Kenneth Taylor in The Living Bible paraphrases the same passage as follows:

> Forgive us our sins, just as we have forgiven those who have sinned against us. . . . Your Heavenly Father will forgive you if you forgive those who sin against you; but if *you* refuse to forgive *them, he* will not forgive *you.*

The Amplified Bible, which does as its title suggests—amplifies and gives new shades of meaning—says:

> Forgive us our debts, as we also have forgiven (left, remitted and let go the debts, and given up resentment against) our debtors. . . . For if you forgive people their trespasses —that is, their reckless and willful sins, leaving them, letting them go and giving up resentment—your heavenly Father will also forgive you.

In seeking God's pardon for our sins, the only thing we have going for us is the satisfaction that was made to the justice of God for sin, by the dying of Christ. There must be a sacrifice to propitiate for sin. I have always especially liked the way this is made so clear in Hebrews 10:

> The old system of Jewish laws gave only a dim foretaste of the good things Christ would do for us. The sacrifices

under the old system were repeated again and again, year after year, but even so they could never save those who lived under their rules. If they could have, one offering would have been enough; the worshipers would have been cleansed once for all, and their feeling of guilt would be done.

But just the opposite happened: those yearly sacrifices reminded them of their disobedience and guilt instead of relieving their minds. *For it is not possible for the blood of bulls and goats really to take away sins.*

That is why Christ said, as he came into the world, "O God, the blood of bulls and goats cannot satisfy you, so you have made ready this body of mine for me to lay as a sacrifice upon your altar. You were not satisfied with the animal sacrifices, slain and burnt before you as offerings for sin." Then I said, "See, I have come to do your will, to lay down my life, just as the Scriptures said that I would."

After Christ said this, about not being satisfied with the various sacrifices and offerings required under the old system, he then added, "Here I am. I have come to give my life."

He cancels the first system in favor of a far better one. *Under this new plan we have been forgiven and made clean by Christ's dying for us once and for all. . . .*[2]

When we pray the Lord's Prayer, we are making a plea not of merit, but purely of grace. To put it plainly, we don't have a leg to stand on unless we are following what Jesus taught. Our responsibility before God if we hope to gain access to heaven is to forbear, forgive, and forget. This is *the* qualification that gives us both God's peace and pardon.

We are to love, accept, and forgive people as individuals, as *a person* for whom Christ died. That man whom you may find it so difficult to forgive is of infinite worth to God. His Son died for that individual.

Francis A. Schaeffer gives eloquent testimony to this dictum in his book *True Spirituality:*

Christianity is not to love in abstraction, but to love the individual who stands before me in a person-to-person relationship. He must never be faceless to me or I am denying everything I say I believe. This concept will always involve some cost: it is not a cheap thing, because we live in a fallen world, and we ourselves are fallen.[3]

How does this work out in the practical down-to-earth aspects of daily living? The disciple Peter wondered about this. He came to Jesus in perplexity and questioned Him concerning this matter. "Sir, how often should I forgive a brother who sins against me? Seven times?"

Perhaps Peter thought he was being magnanimous. Maybe he was recalling Proverbs 24:16, which says that a just man falleth seven times; or perhaps there was remembrance of Amos 2:1, which mentions three transgressions and four that God would no more pass by. Peter knew Christ's previous teaching on forgiveness—the fact that he must not bear a grudge against someone or think about revenge, but he must also forget the injury or injustice.

Did Peter actually think if he had forgiven someone seven times in his lifetime that he could then abandon that person?

Christ quickly set Peter straight. *There is to be no limit to our forgiveness of others.* When He told Peter, "Seventy times seven," He did not mean that literally. Jesus was not saying to forgive someone 490 times and that clears the record for you, but His words are meant to convey the meaning that the number of times we must forgive will be very great.

We have been forgiven so much by God through Christ, how can we possibly be stinting in our forgiveness of others?

Jesus recognized that this would be hard for Peter and the disciples to accept. He decided to make it clearer for them, and so He gave them a parable to show the necessity of forgiveness and the extent to which we must habitually practice this:

The Kingdom of Heaven can be compared to a king who decided to bring his accounts up to date. In the process, one of his debtors was brought in who owed him $10,000,000. He couldn't pay, so the king ordered him sold for the debt, also his wife and children and everything he had.

But the man fell down before the king, his face in the dust, and said, "Oh, sir, be patient with me and I will pay it all."

Then the king was filled with pity for him and released him and forgave his debt.

But when the man left the king, he went to a man who owed him $2,000 and grabbed him by the throat and demanded instant payment.

The man fell down before him and begged him to give him a little time. "Be patient and I will pay it," he pled.

But his creditor wouldn't wait. He had the man arrested and jailed until the debt would be paid in full.

Then the man's friends went to the king and told him what had happened. And the king called before him the man he had forgiven and said, "You evil-hearted wretch! Here I forgave you all that tremendous debt, just because you asked me to—shouldn't you have mercy on others, just as I had mercy on you?"

Then the angry king sent the man to the torture chamber until he had paid every last penny due. So shall my heavenly Father do to you if you refuse to truly forgive your brothers.[4]

What a picture this sets forth of God's pardoning grace! Day by day our debt to God increases; it is beyond all measure, and we have no possible hope of payment. Even if it were possible to live a completely perfect life in the future, we still couldn't cancel out our debt to God; we just don't possess enough goodness or merit on our own, nor could we offer enough in the way of service to fulfill our obligation to Him.

Every sin we commit is a debt to Him. We are truly debtors to God. God keeps an account because He is the righteous Judge of the universe, but every time we claim Christ's sacrifice and His blood, the account is wiped clean. It is as though it never existed. It is our own conscience that must act as the auditor for our souls and our eternal well-being. If we are withholding forgiveness from someone, then the blood of Christ—even though we claim it—will not balance our account.

"If God should deal with us in strict justice, we should be condemned as insolvent debtors." [5] But the God of mercy is ever ready, out of infinite compassion, to forgive us when we humble ourselves seeking forgiveness after having repented. Just as the first debtor in the parable had his debt canceled completely, so God is willing to do that for us. Even though he was pardoned, however, he was still a servant to the king. As such he had an obligation to obedience. We, too, stand in that position.

In stark contrast Jesus described another debtor. His debt by comparison was trifling, yet the first man who had been released from such a great debt was unwilling to show mercy to the man who owed him so little. His severity was totally without reason, particularly since he had just been shown great mercy.

Schaeffer says:

> My fellowman is not unimportant: he is God's image-bearer. That is true of the non-Christian as well as of the Christian. (He is lost, but he is still a man.) Thus when God says, "My child, this sin is different; in this sin you have hurt another person," I respond, "What shall I do, Lord?" And the answer is clear from the Word of God: "Make it right with the man you have hurt. The man you have hurt is not a zero."
>
> But what is the usual reaction when God says to me, "Go and make it right"? It is to answer, "But that would be humiliating." Yet surely, if I have been willing to tell God I am sorry when I have sinned, I must be willing to tell this to the man I have hurt. How can I say, "I am sorry" to God, if I am not willing to say, "I am sorry" to the man I have hurt, when he is my equal, my fellow creature, my

kind? Such a repentance is meaningless hypocrisy. This is
why so many of us have deadness in our lives. We cannot
just trample human relationships and expect our relationship to God to be lovely, beautiful, and open. This is not
only a matter of what is legally right, but of a true relationship of person to person on the basis of who I am and who
the man is.[6]

In the parable Jesus told, we see the smaller debtor's friends
going to bat for him. They inform the king about the unjust
servant's actions. Because the king was a just man who would
not countenance such an unmerciful act, he had his servant,
who owed him such a tremendous debt, thrown into the torture chamber.

The message comes through loud and clear! Those who will
not come to terms with the gospel can expect God's wrath.
"This is how my Heavenly Father will treat you unless you
forgive your brother from your heart." [7]

Jesus told His disciples that day that they must forgive from
their hearts. There is no fooling God. We cannot harbor malice or ill will. We must not plot projects of revenge or allow
hatred to incubate and hatch. God will deny forgiveness to
those who disqualify themselves. It is indispensably necessary
and essential that we forgive others if we hope to be forgiven
by God.

Heaven may, in fact, be small unless the full implication of
what Jesus taught has been grasped by those who in times past
have called themselves Christians and unless those presently
and yet to come will come to grips with the truth that forgiveness in action is something we all must do. Let your life be
an exhibition of the grace of God and His forgiveness. Then
someday you will stand within the portals of heaven looking
into the face of the one Who secured your forgiveness and
assured for you access to the Father for all eternity.

Chapter Notes

Chapter 2

1. Matt. 9:3 (Living Bible).
2. Matt. 9:4–6 (Living Bible).
3. Matt. 9:7 (Living Bible).
4. Matt. 9:8 (Living Bible).
5. Luke 23:34.
6. Luke 23:22.
7. Luke 23:21.
8. Luke 23:17–19 (Living Bible).
9. John 16:2.

Chapter 3

1. Eph. 4:31, 32 (Living Bible).
2. Eph. 4:26, 27 (Living Bible).
3. Eph. 3:14.
4. Eph. 3:16b.

Chapter 4

1. "Up from Suicide," editorial, *Christianity Today,* June 9, 1972.
2. Eph. 4:1–4b, 15, 16 (Living Bible).
3. Eph. 4:12, 13.
4. Matt. 5:21, 22a (Living Bible).
5. Mark 11:22–24 (Living Bible).
6. Isa. 1:4 (Living Bible).
7. Isa. 1:11–15 (Living Bible).
8. I Tim. 2:8 (Living Bible).
9. Acts 2:17 (Living Bible).
10. Isa. 1:16–20 (Living Bible).

Chapter 5

1. Luke 7:36–50.
2. Luke 7:36–38 (Living Bible).
3. Rom. 5.
4. Rom. 4:5.
5. Luke 7:40.
6. *Eternity,* March, 1972.
7. John 16:8.
8. 2 Tim. 3:16–18 (Living Bible).
9. Luke 7:40b (Living Bible).
10. Luke 7:41–43 (Living Bible).
11. Matt. 18:23–35.
12. John 3:16.
13. Ibid.
14. Luke 18:10–14 (Living Bible).
15. Luke 7:44–47 (Living Bible).
16. Luke 7:48 (Living Bible).
17. Luke 7:49 (Living Bible).
18. Luke 7:50 (Living Bible).

Chapter 6

1. Isa. 43:25, 26 (Living Bible).
2. Jer. 31:34 (New American Standard Bible).
3. Heb. 10:17 (New American Standard Bible).
4. Matt. 18:21–35.
5. Ps. 130:3, 4a.
6. Lars Granberg, "Divorce and Remarriage," *Baker's Dictionary of Practical Theology,* ed. by Ralph G. Turnbull (Grand Rapids, Mich.: Baker Book House, 1967).
7. See Helen W. Kooiman, *The Other Side of Divorce.*
8. Eph. 4:32.
9. Henry Wildeboer, "The Minister's Workshop: Rebuilding Marital Fidelity," *Christianity Today,* June 18, 1971.
10. David Augsburger, *70 × 7: The Freedom of Forgiveness* (Chicago: Moody Press, 1970).
11. Matt. 6:15.

Chapter 7

1. James 3:1–13 (Living Bible).
2. Rom. 12:4, 5.
3. Col. 1:14.
4. Col. 1:18.
5. I Pet. 5:8.

6. Ps. 141:3.
7. Ps. 51:15.
8. Gen. 9:20–23 (Living Bible).
9. Matthew Henry.
10. Prov. 14, selected verses (Living Bible).
11. I Pet. 4:8 (Living Bible).
12. Eph. 1:6.
13. Prov. 8:6.
14. Phil. 4:8 (Living Bible).
15. Eph. 5:9 (Living Bible).
16. James 2:12 (Living Bible).
17. Paul S. Rees, *Don't Sleep through the Revolution* (Waco, Tex.: Word Books, 1969).
18. David Augsburger, *70 × 7: The Freedom of Forgiveness* (Chicago: Moody Press, 1970).
19. I Pet. 4:8 (RSV).
20. A. W. Tozer.
21. Matt. 7:1–5.
22. Augsburger, *70 × 7*.
23. Eph. 1:11.
24. Prov. 15:4.
25. Col. 4:6.

Chapter 8

1. Matt. 22:29 (Living Bible).
2. Matt. 22:3b.
3. Matt. 22:22, 33, 34 (Living Bible).
4. Robert H. Schuller, *Self-love: The Dynamic Force of Success* (New York: Hawthorn, 1969).
5. Matt. 22:36–40 (Living Bible).
6. Rom. 13:8–10 (Living Bible).
7. George Otis, *Like a Roaring Lion* (Van Nuys, Calif.: Time-Light, 1973).
8. Ibid.
9. Matt. 6:14.
10. Ps. 103:3, 12.
11. Harold J. Sala, *Guidelines for Peace of Mind* (Redondo Beach, Calif.).
12. Matt. 9:2b.
13. Luke 4:18, 19 (Living Bible).
14. Maxwell Maltz, *Psycho-Cybernetics* (Englewood Cliffs, N.J.: Prentice-Hall, 1969).
15. Ibid.
16. Schuller, *Self-love*.

Chapter 9

1. David Augsburger, *Be All You Can Be* (Wheaton, Ill.: Creation House, 1970).
2. Michael Esses, *Michael, Michael, Why Do You Hate Me?* (Plainfield, N.J.: Logos International, 1973).
3. Luke 15:13–16 (Living Bible).
4. Luke 15:17–19 (Living Bible).
5. Luke 15:18.
6. Ps. 7:16.
7. Luke 15:17–20 (Living Bible).
8. Luke 15:22–24.
9. Isa. 61:10 (Living Bible).
10. Eph. 6:15 (Amplified Bible).
11. Isa. 52:7 (Living Bible).
12. 2 Chron. 6:41b.
13. Luke 15:26, 27 (Living Bible).
14. Luke 15:28.
15. Luke 15:29, 30 (Living Bible).
16. Luke 15:31, 32 (Living Bible).

Chapter 10

1. Eph. 4:21–24 (Amplified Bible).
2. Eph. 4:18.
3. Eph. 5:1.
4. Eph. 4:24b (Living Bible).
5. Eph. 4:25–32.
6. Eph. 5:1, 2 (Phillips).

Chapter 11

1. 1 Cor. 2:9.
2. John Hunter, *Knowing God's Secrets* (Grand Rapids, Mich.: Zondervan, 1965).
3. Phil. 4:4.
4. 2 Tim. 1:12.
5. Acts 9:14.
6. Acts 9:4, 5 (Living Bible).
7. Acts 9:5.
8. Phil. 4:13 (Amplified Bible).

Chapter 12

1. Lev. 20:10, Deut. 22:22–24, John 8:5.
2. John 8:6.
3. John 8:7b (Amplified Bible).
4. Helen W. Kooiman, *The Other Side of Divorce*.

5. David Augsburger, *70 × 7: The Freedom of Forgiveness* (Chicago: Moody Press, 1970).
6. Col. 3:12–14 (Phillips).
7. Ps. 32:1.
8. Charles L. Allen, *The Touch of the Master's Hand* (Old Tappan, N.J.: Fleming H. Revell, 1966).
9. Eugenia Price, *The Unique World of Women* (Grand Rapids, Mich.: Zondervan, 1969).
10. John 8:11 (Amplified Bible).
11. Matt. 7:1, 2.
12. Rom. 14:10–13 (Amplified Bible).
13. James 4:11–12 (Amplified Bible).
14. Lev. 19:16.

Chapter 13

1. Keith Miller, *Habitation of Dragons* (Waco, Tex.: Word Books, 1970).
2. 1 Sam. 16:6, 7 (New American Standard Bible).
3. Isa. 11:3.
4. 2 Cor. 13:5.
5. Prov. 28:13.
6. H. S. Vigeveno, *Sinners Anonymous* (Waco, Tex.: Word Books, 1970).
7. Dietrich Bonhoeffer, *Life Together* (New York: Harper & Row, 1954).
8. Ps. 32:1–6 (Living Bible).
9. John Scott, *Confess Your Sins* (Philadelphia: Westminster, 1973).
10. Ps. 90:8 (Amplified Bible).
11. James 5:16 (RSV).
12. Bonhoeffer, *Life Together.*
13. Harold J. Sala, *Guidelines for Peace of Mind* (Redondo Beach, Calif.: Guidelines, 1973).
14. 1 Pet. 5:7.
15. David Augsburger, *70 × 7: The Freedom of Forgiveness* (Chicago: Moody Press, 1970).

Chapter 14

1. Matt. 12:35.
2. Matt. 12:33.
3. Matt. 12:33–37 (Living Bible).
4. Prov. 25:26, 26:22–24 (Amplified Bible).
5. Matt. 15:18, 19, 20a (Living Bible).
6. Prov. 18:21.
7. Matt. 12:37 (Amplified Bible).
8. Ralph Bell, "Forgiveness: The Great Liberator," *Alliance Witness,* March 15, 1972.
9. 1 Sam. 16:13.
10. 1 Sam. 17:40–47.

11. 1 Sam. 17:42 (Living Bible).
12. 1 Sam. 17:45–47 (Living Bible).
13. 1 Sam. 18:14 (Living Bible).
14. Ps. 4:7.
15. John 14:27 (Living Bible).
16. Ps. 5:4–6 (Amplified Bible).
17. J. Oswald Sanders, *Spiritual Manpower* (Chicago: Moody Press, 1965).
18. Ps. 51 (Living Bible).
19. 2 Sam. 12:13b, 14.
20. Rom. 2:23, 24 (Living Bible).
21. 2 Sam. 24:1–3.
22. 2 Sam. 24:10 (Living Bible).
23. 2 Sam. 24:14 (Living Bible).
24. Sanders, *Spiritual Manpower.*

Chapter 15

1. James 1:27 (Living Bible).
2. 1 Tim. 5:16 (Living Bible).
3. 1 Tim. 5:8 (Living Bible).
4. Matt. 23:14a.
5. Exod. 21:24–25.
6. Lev. 24:17–22.
7. Deut. 19:21.
8. Matt. 5:38–48 (Living Bible).
9. Phil. 3:12–15a (Living Bible).
10. John 18:22.
11. 1 Pet. 2:23 (Phillips).

Chapter 16

1. Matt. 6:12, 14, 15 (Phillips).
2. Heb. 10:1–10 (Living Bible). Italics mine.
3. Francis A. Schaeffer, *True Spirituality* (Wheaton, Ill.: Tyndale House, 1971).
4. Matt. 18:23–24 (Living Bible).
5. Matthew Henry.
6. Schaeffer, *True Spirituality.*
7. Matt. 18:35 (Phillips).

HELEN KOOIMAN has had a varied career in the world of communications and the world of books. From 1952 to 1970 she founded, co-owned, and managed two Christian bookstores in Bellflower and Buena Park, California. Then she became TV scriptwriter for Dr. Leighton Ford of the Billy Graham Evangelistic Association. Simultaneously she served as editorial assistant to the president of Christian Freedom Foundation in Buena Park, California. She left the latter post in April 1972 to become communications director and scriptwriter for daily religious and inspirational broadcasts for Haven of Rest in Hollywood.

She began writing seriously one day after she read the little booklet "My Heart, Christ's Home" and became convinced of the need to turn her hobby over to the Lord for His use. Quickly she gathered heaps of slips on which she had been gathering the sayings and doings of her children and began writing a woman's column for her church's periodical, a column that eventually became the book *Please Pray for the Cabbages*.

Among her many activities are the following: featured author and speaker at Christian Bookseller's Conventions in Chicago, Cincinnati, and San Diego; lecturer for Norm Rohrer's Southern California Christian Writer's Guild School of Writing; speaker at churches, conferences, conventions, clubs, and luncheons on inspirational themes; wrote and recorded a series of twenty-nine radio scripts for the Christian Bookseller's Association; guest and lecturer for Billy Graham's DECISION School of Writing in Minneapolis.

Her many successful books include: *Silhouettes: Women behind Great Men; Transformed: Behind the Scenes with Billy Graham; Living Words of Comfort and Cheer; Cameos: Women Fashioned by God; Small Talk; Please Pray for the Cabbages; Joyfully Expectant: Meditations before the Baby Comes; Walter Knott: Keeper of the Flame*.

2283